# weird CARS

# weird
# CARS

## A CENTURY OF THE WORLD'S STRANGEST CARS

**SECOND EDITION**

# STEPHEN VOKINS

**Dedication**
This book is dedicated with my sincere thanks to the staff of the
Hospital for Sick Children, Great Ormond Street, London, without
whose dedication and care I would not be here.

© Stephen Vokins 2012

First edition published in 2004
This second edition published in 2012

A catalogue record for this book is available from the British Library

ISBN 978 0 85733 237 0

Library of Congress catalog card no. 2011943927

Published by Haynes Publishing,
Sparkford, Yeovil, Somerset, BA22 7JJ, UK

Tel: 01963 442030 Fax: 01963 440001
Int. tel: +44 1963 442030 Int. fax: +44 1963 440001
E-mail: sales@haynes.co.uk
Web site: www.haynes.co.uk

Haynes North America, Inc.,
861 Lawrence Drive, Newbury Park,
California 91320, USA

Edited by Sophie Blackman
Design and Layout by Dominic Stickland

Printed in the USA by Odcombe Press LP,
1299 Bridgestone Parkway, La Vergne, TN 37086

# Contents

# Foreword by Lord Montagu of Beaulieu

The history of the motor vehicle is a fascinating topic, and for many people, among whom I number myself, it is a lifetime passion. The internal combustion engine has changed the way much of the globe functions, and its influence is still spreading, with huge growth predicted in China in the next two decades. To those who claim it has ruined our towns and countryside, it is worth pointing out that had we continued to rely on the horse as the principal means of transport, we would by now be under several feet of waste product of a rather more organic nature than the pollution problems we currently face.

The number of individuals and companies who have at some stage indulged in car manufacture to a greater or lesser extent reaches well into the thousands, whilst the number of different car designs is a multiple of that, and so it should come as no surprise to find that amongst this huge multitude, there are some eccentric and weird machines worthy of a moment in the limelight. This book highlights more than 250 examples of independent thought, and serious experimentation, much of which sadly resulted in evolutionary cul-de-sacs, and celebrates the blood, sweat and tears that went into their manufacture.

The work of the creators of the cars featured in the following pages merits recognition, and whilst with the benefit of hindsight some of the resultant vehicles are genuinely amusing, this does not in any way take away from the vision of their creators. To the lover of all things automotive, the failures are as rewarding to read about as the successes with which we are all familiar, and contained in this book are some long-forgotten, and in several cases, never-before-written-about machines which will delight and excite.

*Montagu of Beaulieu*

# Introduction

There is popular myth circulating on the internet which concerns the demise of a resident of Arizona, who, having obtained an ex-military JATO (jet-assisted take-off) rocket engine, normally used to help planes take off from aircraft carriers, fixed it to his 1967 Chevrolet Impala and headed out into the desert to test his new supercar. Having accelerated as fast as the car would normally be expected to go, the driver, and soon-to-be-pilot, ignited the rocket engine, propelling the hapless Chevy to a speed approaching 350mph. However, just five seconds later, 2.5 miles further on, things started to go badly wrong. With a bend in the road rapidly approaching, he applied the brakes, which, being hopelessly inadequate for the task now facing them, immediately and completely melted. For good measure, the tyres also let go, leaving thick black rubber marks on the road surface. At this point, the car became airborne, and 1.4 miles later, impacted into a cliff face leaving a blackened crater three feet deep in the rock.

Whilst this car, the truth of which is hard to verify, does not appear in the following pages, there are many other very silly, and in some cases, equally daft cars to enjoy. Designing a car is not an easy process, and there are many failures for every one that succeeds. When conceiving a new design there are many rules to obey, following the initial inspiration. In addition to legislation on driver and passenger safety and any local laws for the car's intended market, there are also a huge number of conventions of design that need to be adhered to if the car is to be sufficiently appealing for the public to buy it in quantities that will make it a commercial success.

One such convention, for instance, states that a car should have four wheels (although three may be acceptable in exceptional circumstances), and that these four wheels should be arranged in pairs: one at the front in control of steering and most of the braking, and the second pair at the rear. Now, while such a view

makes obvious sense to virtually everybody, there are those who have felt the need to question it, and sometimes in a bewildering way. The results of trying to re-invent the wheel (or car) can produce some thoroughly eccentric machines, and featured in these pages are more than 250 of the world's weirdest.

While no-one could rightly argue that designing a successful car is a simple process, following the rules at least makes the task a logical progression. The designers of the cars included in this book were, by and large, a far braver (or perhaps less hidebound) group of people, who chose to wander from the path, and were convinced that convention had it all wrong. They followed their beliefs, putting their money where their mouths were, hoping to change the way we looked at and used cars. The vehicles they brought to market were generally unsuccessful, and often brought about the bankruptcy of their creators. With very few exceptions, all of the cars included were serious attempts at car design, and the temptation to feature novelty or gimmick cars such as the road-going sofa or garden shed has been largely resisted. It is easy to laugh with the benefit of hindsight and from the comfort of one's couch at the often bizarre designs that frequently set out to ask the questions no-one had even thought to ask, but these are cars that their creators wholeheartedly believed in.

The aim of this book is not to scoff but to applaud and to celebrate the achievements, the diversity of approach to problems faced by all car makers, and their attendant results with the cars they built, however ridiculous they may now appear. So read on, and be glad that the cars we own and use today are as 'normal' as they are. If the history of car design can be viewed in Darwinian terms, then contained in these pages are the weird machines rejected along the evolutionary path that has led us to today's fine, but largely characterless machines.

# In the beginning

# Bersey Electric

It is tempting to think that electric cars represent the future, or at least, will have an important role to play. What is perhaps surprising to realise, however, is that well over 100 years ago, car designers were thinking along exactly the same lines.

Walter Bersey was an electrical engineer in London who built his first electric bus in 1886, and was building electric cars in 1895. To call them cars is possibly stretching a point: they were horseless carriages powered by electric motors. Three of his vehicles competed in the first Brighton Run of 1896, although, as Bersey later confessed, they went most of the way by train.

# Bjering Bedelia

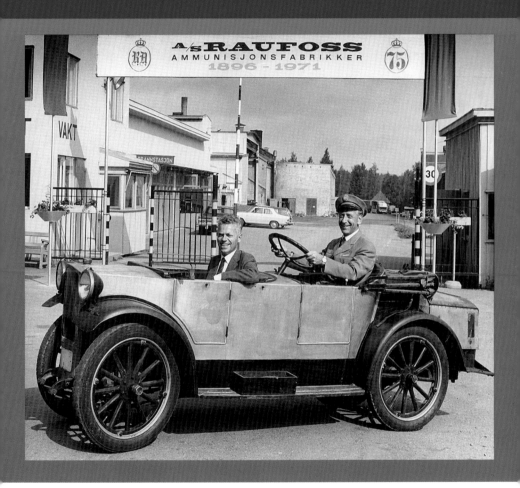

Many of the world's weirdest cars were built with a specific purpose in mind, and the Bjering Bedelia from Holland was no exception.

In production for just two years after the end of the First World War, the Bedelia's main purpose was that of a country police car. To that end, Bjering designed it so that the driver sat in an elevated position behind the passenger, pillion style. So, assuming the passenger was a villain under arrest and on his way to the police station, the driver, being behind and sitting higher up, could keep an eye on both the road ahead and on his unwilling passenger.

# Bow-V-Car

Designed in Luton, England by Charles Beauvais, the Bow-V-Car had a strange name in keeping with its weird nature. The company he set up in 1922 to build his three-wheeler, the Plycar Company Ltd, gave a pretty good hint as to the car's principal building material. Its integral body and chassis were built of plywood and featured a porthole in the side of the bonnet admitting light from the external lamp to illuminate the dashboard.

Although there was a ready market for cheap cars from people recently demobbed after the First World War, very few Bow-V-Cars were sold and the company folded after trading for only one year.

# Dunkley Moke

The Dunkley Moke, built in Birmingham in the final years of the 19th century, is without doubt, one of the weirdest cars ever to make it into production. With four wheels arranged in a diamond pattern, the largest pair, being placed in the middle, were responsible for driving the contraption, while either the front or rear wheel took care of steering it. As only one of these two differently sized wheels could be on the ground at any one time, the issue of which steered the car was determined by the location of the heaviest of the two people needed to drive it.

Undertaking a journey on a Moke was very much a team effort, with the front person in charge of steering, whilst bizarrely, braking was the job of the backwards facing passenger.

While patently ridiculous in so many ways, the Dunkley was at least a whole century ahead of its time in one important way: its engine ran on (town) gas rather than petrol. There are no records showing how many Dunkley Mokes were sold, although it is believed that the number must have been (thankfully) in single figures.

# Gasi

The Gasi from Berlin was a strange three-wheeler which was only available for a short period in 1921. Its two-seater body accommodated its occupants in tandem style, but for some reason, which is not immediately obvious, the driver actually sat behind the passenger.

The two-cylinder air-cooled engine was positioned in front of the passenger, and the single front wheel hinted at motorcycle origins. No-one should have been surprised that such a machine was destined for a very short life.

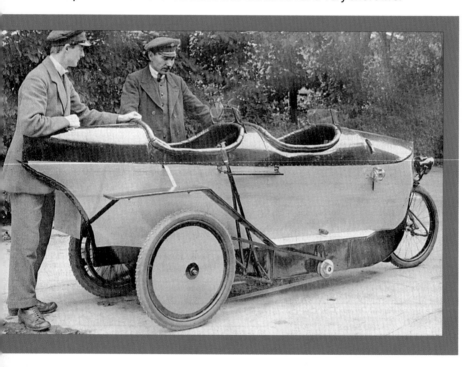

# Hanomag

The Hanomag was a German economy vehicle with a difference: it was one of very few cars ever put into full production with a wickerwork body of which several hundred were made, alongside a (slightly) more conventional metal-bodied design. It was sold between 1924 and 1928.

Cheapness was guaranteed courtesy of a rear-mounted 500cc water-cooled engine, while the fuel tank and spare wheel were located at the front. In total, nearly 16,000 examples were built, but very few survive today.

# Hidromobile

It's tempting to think that most silly ideas for cars are relatively modern, but hopefully this book will go some way to dispel that myth. Back in 1914, for example, W.C. Mazzei from New York dreamt up the Hidromobile, and persuaded a corporation in Los Angeles that it was a good idea for them to build it. It isn't known how many were built beyond the example in this photograph, which featured in an article in *Popular Electricity and Modern Mechanics*, but the accompanying text was particularly praising of Mattei's ingenuity, and thought the vehicle ideal 'for use by travellers who must cross streams and flooded areas.' For the time, its bodywork was remarkably streamlined, but history does not record whether this attribute helped it either in or out of the water, and no examples are known to have survived.

Marcel Leyat was an inventor based on the Côte d'Azur, whose legacy is among the most bizarre. Both before and after the First World War he was involved in attempting to adapt aircraft technology to cars. While making cars streamlined and light is undeniably a smart move, attaching a huge propeller to the front was probably not. This worked inasmuch as the car moved forwards, but apart from the obvious safety issues addressed in part by covering the front with a wire mesh grille, it made for a horribly noisy and draughty experience for the occupants, whilst the windscreen was quickly covered in dust, oil, and everything else the propeller could throw at it. Steered by its rear wheels, several examples were made, but it was never taken unduly seriously.

# Marks-Moir

Most people, when questioned, struggle to think of more than one Australian car manufacturer, Holden. This is unfortunate, because by 1940 there had already been around 70 attempts to launch motor car businesses there, and one of them, the Marks-Moir, was definitely worthy of note, especially to the devotee of quirkiness.

Designed in 1923 by W.A. Moir, these cars were equipped with a limited-slip differential, and over the years used a variety of engines, mounted transversely mid-ships. It was their bodywork, however, that was most unusual, being made from stitched and glued waterproof plywood. Contrary to one's expectations, the resulting monocoque was immensely stiff and well suited to the task, having been conceived originally for the building of boats. The company lasted from 1923 to 1928.

# Mauser Einspur-Auto

The Mauser Einspur-Auto was a crazy design which first saw the light of day when exhibited as a prototype in 1921 at the Berlin Motor Show, and made it into production two years later.

Once in motion, the two balance wheels would lift up, converting the weird machine into a two-wheeler manoeuvred by quite the largest steering wheel ever seen on a road-going vehicle. It was powered by a single-cylinder 500cc engine and was capable of carrying three people, with two passengers sitting side by side behind the driver.

After its initial failure, the design was resurrected as the Monotrace, which survived until 1930.

In 1923, Oliver D. North, who was chief engineer at Scammell Lorries in Putney, approached Ralph Lucas for the finance to build a car of his own extremely unorthodox design. Clad in an aluminium body with a fabric roof, this lightweight machine was influenced by the streamlined designs of Edmund Rumpler, and was powered by a rear-mounted five-cylinder 1,460cc engine.

It took the ideas of low weight and aerodynamic efficiency very seriously, but, as neither Lucas nor North had any production facilities, only one car was ever built, and eventually, after five years, it was broken up.

# Parker Bushbury

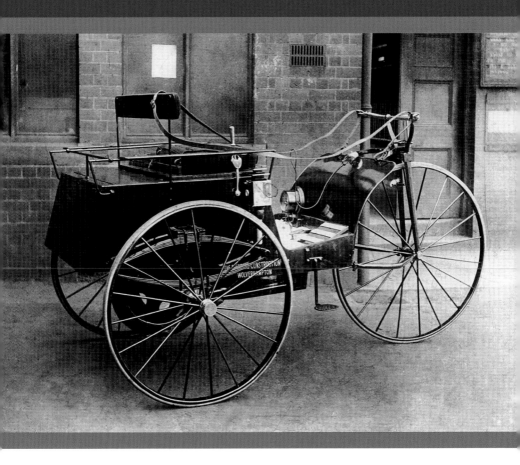

At the dawn of motoring, many people referred to the new inventions that crawled out on to the roads of the world as 'horseless carriages', mainly because carriages were what they were used to seeing, and many looked like carriages whose horse had been given the afternoon off. Of no car could that be truer, however, than the electrically powered 1897 Parker Bushbury, made in Wolverhampton, Staffordshire. Instead of a steering wheel, or even a more primitive tiller bar, the makers equipped the spindly carriage with reins for the driver to steer it. It is not known how many were built, but the number was doubtless very small.

# Pennington Autocar

In days of old when men were bold and road safety was not yet an issue, a character called Edward Joel Pennington, described by many as a charlatan, designed and built his New Patent Autocar in the UK.

Perhaps because he realised he would be called upon to demonstrate it at some stage, he placed the driver at the very rear of the machine, behind the single rear wheel and as far away as possible from any likely accident damage. He even proposed seating four passengers sideways along the length of the machine to boost its human cargo-carrying capacity. Only five vehicles were built, one of which was entered in the 1896 Emancipation Run from London to Brighton. It failed to complete the trip when one of its claimed 'unpuncturable tyres' burst.

# Rumpler Tropfenwagen

The Rumpler Tropfenwagen (tear-drop car), first seen at the 1921 Berlin Motor Show, was a fascinating machine, which apart from its startlingly futuristic and streamlined shape, also offered a W6 engine, with three banks of paired cylinders all working on a common crankshaft.

The engine was placed at the rear of the body, the design of which had been heavily influenced by Rumpler's earlier work in the aircraft industry. Around 80 cars were built, but sales were slow, and ultimately, a number ended up being used as taxis in Berlin; their high price of RM17,000 putting off many would-be purchasers who had not been not dissuaded by its styling.

# Singer Motor Wheel

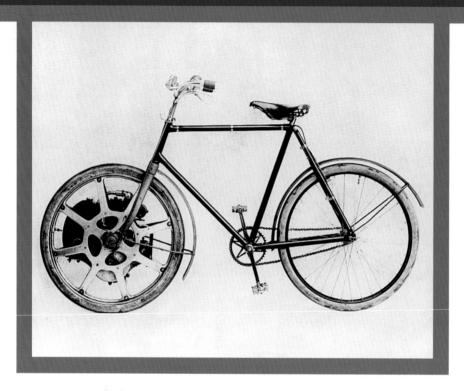

The Singer cycle firm of Coventry entered the car-making business by acquiring the manufacturing rights of the Perks & Birch Motor Wheel in 1901, and attaching their wheel to the front of a tricycle, an arrangement which carried on until 1907, by which time they were producing conventional cars.

The Motor Wheel-equipped tricycles were marketed as tricars, and enabled the driver/rider to control the contraption from the normal position, while on some examples they could accommodate two further passengers facing rearwards in a basket arrangement fixed behind the driver.

# Sunbeam-Mabley

The Sunbeam-Mabley was the work of an ornamental iron-work designer from Wolverhampton, which may go some way to explaining certain details on this most unusual carriage built between 1901 and 1904. The driver sat at the back, presumably because he would be a chauffeur and should not, therefore, expect to go ahead of his employer. The front passengers faced the offside of the road, rather than forwards, and there was only just enough room for two adults on this seat. Weirder still, allegedly in an attempt to prevent skidding, its wheels were arranged in a diamond pattern, with the front and rear ones both steering, courtesy of a tiller. This gave the car very sensitive steering, which was not easy to master, especially on the rough roads over which it would have to travel back in 1901. Perhaps its top speed of just 12mph was no bad thing, as attempts to control it at higher speeds would doubtless have brought disastrous results.

It had a 2½hp De Dion engine mounted at the front of the car and this drove the centre pair of wheels. Possibly the greatest surprise of all, however, was that it sold very well at £130, with several hundred examples finding homes in the two years the car was offered.

# Thames Motor Coach

The Thames Ironworks, Shipbuilding & Engineering Co. Ltd, whose social club eventually became Millwall Football Club, made, as their name suggests, a wide range of things, but in 1911, they took an order from Motor Coaches Ltd to build a fleet of mock stage-coaches, whose styling echoed that of horse-drawn carriages from the previous century.

This seemingly absurd order was for a very specific purpose: they were used to take people from London to race-courses at Ascot and Epsom, with the wealthy riding inside while their servants would shiver in the open on top. Once at the racecourse, the wealthy would then go up on top, using the unusual machine as a grandstand from which to view the day's proceedings.

Powered by a 5-litre engine, it was much slower than one might expect from such a powerplant, and with heavy wooden wheels and solid tyres, was not only way behind the times, but it must surely have been an uncomfortable ride for the exposed servants and the driver, and also for the better-seated passengers inside.

# Small isn't necessarily beautiful

# Acoma Super Comtesse

The French firm of Acoma (1975–84) was very successful, selling 3,500 cars a year. The cars they built, however, were far from ordinary: they specialised in making a variety of weird microcars, nearly all using 50cc Motobecane moped engines. Early examples were three-wheelers, with the front wheel doing the driving, but later examples, such as the hugely funny Super Comtesse from 1979, had four wheels. These were tiny, however, and combined with a tall polyester body, made for an unstable vehicle. It was at its safest when in slow-moving traffic.

# All Cars Charly

So much more than just a silly name, the All Cars Charly was built in Italy from 1978 to 1985, having been bought from its original manufacturer, Autozodiaco. Powered by a 49cc moped engine, its triangular-shaped plastic body, sitting rather high on its three wheels gave it the appearance of an off-road Bond Bug that had been somewhat squashed. As was common among microcars, luxury was sparse and accommodation cramped, with progress best described as modest.

# Allard Clipper

The Clipper from 1955 can, at best, be called unusual. A three-wheeled machine powered by a 346cc, 8bhp Villiers motorcycle engine clothed in a glassfibre body, it was claimed it could seat three adults abreast, with a further two children finding uncomfortable seating in the boot, which hid a dickey seat. Sadly for the Clipper, its problems didn't stop with trying to persuade people to love this ugly duckling: it was also hopelessly unreliable, suffering from cooling difficulties and weak drive shafts. In the end, a pilot batch of 20 was built, and only two are known to survive.

# Avolette

The French Avolette was a three-wheeler which owed much of its design to the Brutsch Mopetta. Available in four body styles, all made from glassfibre, it came with a choice of engines ranging from 125cc to 250cc, which drove the rear wheel by means of a chain.

When fully equipped with white-wall tyres and chrome fittings, as seen in this example on display at The Bruce Weiner Microcar Museum, it was an inoffensive-looking, albeit undeniably small machine. Its appeal was further enhanced by the fact that the smaller-engined machines could be driven without the need for a driving licence. It was, however, short-lived, being in production form 1956 to 1957.

# Bel Motors Veloto

The Veloto (1974–80) was an incredibly crude machine, even by the standards of the microcar class to which it belonged. Powered by a 50cc moped engine, it was the first two-seater that was legal for a 14-year-old to drive in its home country of France. The rear wheels were driven via an automatic transmission to a not-too-frightening maximum speed of just 25mph.

Its scant glassfibre bodywork was available in a variety of primary colours, while the large hood which can only have impeded yet further the lamentably slow progress, was only available in black. Approximately 100 were built.

# Brutsch Mopetta

Egon Brutsch was a German racing driver who convinced himself, if no-one else, that the world needed small cars – really small cars. His Mopetta, built in his home town of Stuttgart, was launched in 1951 and subsequently exhibited at the 1956 Earls Court Motor Show. It was just 5ft 7in long, and was probably the smallest car ever proposed for serious production.

Its glassfibre bodywork resembled a cross between a fairground dodgem car and an egg into which the driver had to lower himself like getting into a bath, before unleashing the 49cc engine's power through one of the rear wheels. Although it never went into production, the prototype still survives.

# Casalini Sulky

Microcars, in general, are weird cars, but the Sulky from Italy merits special mention, not least because of its amusing name. Perhaps it was so named because anyone forced to be seen travelling in one was likely to be in a questionable mood for days afterwards, or perhaps it was aimed at sulky teenagers without full driving licences.

Launched at the end of the 1970s, it came with either a 50cc or 60cc engine, and unusually for microcars, the bodywork was all-steel mounted on a tubular chassis, although the usual scant effort appears to have been made in giving it a pleasing appearance.

# Citroën Lacoste

Citroën are a company with a long and distinguished history of delivering the unexpected to the motoring world. Therefore no one should have been surprised when, at the Paris Motor Show of 2010, they pulled the wraps off the Lacoste – a co-venture with the French fashion house of the same name. It resembled, in the words of one UK magazine, the offspring of a 'one-night stand between a golf buggy and a Mini Moke.' Whilst it lacked both doors and a roof, its designers had thought about what to do when it rains – a yellow hood automatically inflates to protect the occupants. Power came from a three-cylinder petrol engine, and a full set of Lacoste accessories would be available, should the patently mad decision to make the car ever be taken. It wasn't.

Small isn't necessarily beautiful

# Colliday Chariot

Launched in 1965, this was another attempt at marrying a scooter with a car to provide high levels of economy whilst offering more comfort than that of a two-wheel machine. It cost £300 (less than half the price of a Mini), had a turning circle of 7ft, and a top speed of 'over 30mph'.

The engine and transmission were mounted on the front wheel which, because it was able to turn through 360°, meant that no reverse gear was needed. Inside the cabin there were just two pedals: one marked 'STOP' and the other 'GO'. Crude, cheap and ugly, it found no buyers in Britain or anywhere else.

Many of the world's weirdest cars have come from that peculiar school of design known as microcars, but few can equal the 1979 Flipper from France for sheer bizarre appearance.

With its amphibious looks, there must have been a temptation for the driver to head for the nearest river – and leave it there. Its front wheels did the driving, and being capable of turning through 360°, it had no need for a reverse gear to add complication to its moped engine and transmission. Most amusingly, its designers, perhaps in a moment of self-doubt, equipped it with emergency cycle pedals in case of breakdown.

# Kleinschnittger

The Kleinschnittger was one of Germany's more successful microcars, with over 3,000 examples built, and was on sale for a period of seven years from 1950 onwards. It was a basic machine, however, with its front wheels driven by a 125cc engine and its two occupants enjoying minimal concessions to comfort from its open body.

# Larmar

The Larmar from Essex was one of the narrowest cars of all time, and with good reason: its 28½in width was to enable the weird-looking machine, whose principal intended clientele were invalids, to fit through doorways.

Launched in 1946 for £198, there was a significant number of potential customers who had been injured during the war. It originally came with a 250cc engine, later enlarged to 350cc, was capable of 35mph, had a turning circle of 15ft and was equipped with a folding hood to keep its solitary occupant dry. It sold only in small numbers, and production ceased in 1951.

# Leata Sedan

Donald Stinebaugh of Post Falls, Idaho, when launching his claim to automotive manufacture in 1975, touchingly named the diminutive, retro-styled car after his wife Leata, although it is to be hoped that Mrs Stinebaugh was better proportioned than the dumpy little car that carried her name.

It had a 50bhp engine which gave a top speed of 70mph and 55mpg fuel consumption. Selling for $2,895, the strange attempt at retro-styling fell over badly with its hugely oversized wheels, which made the whole car look like a child's pedal-car, and sales were poor as a result.

# Ligier JS4

Guy Ligier had been building sports cars in France for a decade when he started producing microcars, and the JS4 from 1980, named after his racing driver friend Jo Schlesser who had died some years previously, soon became the best-selling car in this sector of the market.

Early examples were powered by a 50cc moped engine, but other engine options subsequently became available up to a 347cc diesel engine. Although no-one could claim that its all-steel bodywork (unusual in the microcar class) was pretty, it proved to be surprisingly popular, achieving sales of over 7,000. Allegedly, it could be driven safely, even if one of the wheels fell off – what a claim!

# MT

The MT was a tiny two-seater microcar built in Barcelona in 1955. Apart from its weird, strangely proportioned body supported on three wheels, there was little to distinguish it from many other microcars, except that it had more than just the most basic of equipment. It had an electric starter and a proper folding roof, and an attempt was made to make the front look like that of a conventional car.

Standing at the side of the road looking at this daft machine, a comedian might be tempted to ask whether this car was half full, or half MT.

# Outspan Orange

When Alec Issigonis et al set about designing the Mini in the late 1950s they could never have guessed just how successful it would become, or how many other cars would rely on its mechanicals as their basis. Even if they had been able to hazard a guess, they could never have foreseen the Outspan Orange, which must be one of the weirdest cars ever to take to the road.

Designed and built by Brian Waite Enterprises of Bodiam, East Sussex in 1972, a small fleet of these top-heavy machines was made, rather obviously to promote the fruit, and they travelled the cities and fairs of the world for many years successfully attracting attention. Due to the short wheelbase and high body, they were frighteningly unstable, and could easily reward unwisely spirited driving or fierce braking with a terminal roll. Several survive however, including one on show at the National Motor Museum, Beaulieu.

# Peugeot BB1

In the words of Peugeot's Marketing Department introducing the BB1, 'Peugeot has fearlessly pushed back the conventions and boundaries of automobile manufacturing to bring a totally original response to the current and future needs of urban mobility. Capable of seating four people in a vehicle just 2.5 metres long, the BB1 concept car is a full electric vehicle that reinvents the automobile in every way: architecture, style, interior design, drive, connectivity – while all the time respecting the environment.' They appear, however, to have overlooked that most basic of virtues – good looks.

The Rovin D3 3CV two-seater, to give it its full title, was launched by Robert and Raoul de Rovin in France in 1948, and it looked very much like a dodgem car from a fairground ride. A 425cc flat-twin engine placed in the back propelled the little machine around up to a top speed of just 40mph. Just under 1,000 examples were built.

# Russon Minicar

Most cars are designed by car designers, or at least, engineers, but in the case of the Russon Minicar, the design team responsible was the editorial staff of *Aeromodeller* magazine, based in Bedfordshire and headed by D.A. Russell, the managing editor.

Its claimed top speed of 50mph was ambitious, while 65mpg may well have been possible, should anyone have been sufficiently determined to stay with the car for long enough. It had dangerously inefficient rod-and-cable brakes, a 250cc Excelsior motorcycle engine and three-speed gearbox hidden at the rear. In total, less than 10 Minicars were built during 1951–52. None survive.

# Rytecraft Scootacar

Designed by Jack Shillan and built by the British Motorboat Manufacturing Co. Ltd of London, the Rytecraft Scootacar started life as an electric-powered fairground ride tethered to a central pole, until he fitted a 98cc Villiers Midget petrol engine. The minuscule machine was then allowed to make its way on to the King's Highway, where in 1934, there were no Construction & Use regulations or MoT tests to prevent such folly. Early examples had only one gear (no reverse), no springing beyond its balloon tyres, no electric starter or electric lights, and were capable of only 15mph.

As time passed, it gained three forward gears and a reverse, lights, electric horn, better brakes and a 250cc engine which trebled the car's top speed to 45mph and gave 80mpg. At £80, it was marketed as 'Britain's smallest and lowest-priced motor car' and over 1,000 examples were sold. It is not known how many survive.

Small isn't necessarily beautiful

# Scootacar

The first impression of the Scootacar is that someone should have taken Henry Brown, the car's designer, to one side and quietly suggested he considered devoting his life to something else, or at least ask him to take a long hard look at the car and see if he couldn't do better.

Being light, it was capable of a very pleasing 80mpg, and for those not put off by the fear of ridicule, must have been a tempting proposition as an alternative to public transport. Priced at £287 6s 8d including purchase tax, it was advertised as 'The covered scooter with a car-sized door.' Frighteningly, some of the later Scootacars, named mischievously 'De Luxe Twin', came equipped with a 324cc Villiers engine which could see the startled owners propelled to a death-defying 68mph.

The three-wheeler Scootacar, launched in 1957 and built by Hunslet Engineering in Leeds, remained on sale for seven years, eventually selling roughly 1,500 examples.

# Soletta

The Soletta was a strange machine that looked, in certain areas, like a hideously malformed version of Alec Issigonis's Austin 1100/1300 range. Built in Switzerland, it was launched at the 1956 Geneva Motor Show and sported a glassfibre two-door body. It was powered by a 750cc air-cooled motorcycle engine placed amidships, and was capable of 62mph.

# Tourette

The Tourette was built by the Progress Supreme Co. of Purley, Surrey, which normally made motor scooters. Launched in 1956, it was propelled by a 197cc two-stroke Villiers engine, and it had four forward gears, and 'Dynastart', which allowed the engine to be started in reverse, thus endowing the ugly machine with four forward and four reverse gears. According to the sales brochure, it would cruise 'happily' at 40–45mph, with a top speed of 55mph, and would return 90mpg if driven carefully. The company even offered a hand-operated clutch conversion free of charge to any disabled would-be owner. Only 26 examples were ever made and it is not known if any survive.

The Triver was an ugly bubblecar from Spain, whose manufacturer, Construcciones Acoracadas in Bilbao in 1952, was more usually employed making strong-boxes and safes; a fact which goes some way to explaining the strength of build and the metal used in the panels being a full 3mm thick. This naturally brought with it weight problems and lethargic performance.

Capable of carrying up to four people including the driver, it measured less than 11ft in length, and the later versions, fitted at the rear with a Hispano-Villiers 14bhp engine, managed a top speed of 48mph.

# Volugrafo Bimbo

The Italian Volugrafo Bimbo of 1946 was advertised as 'the smallest car in the world', which, strangely, doesn't actually incite many people instinctively to rush out wanting to buy one. Its power came from a 125cc 5bhp engine, and its body, which looked not unlike a dodgem car (aided by its diminutive size and lack of doors) was made from aluminium.

# Waaijenberg Canta

The Waaijenberg Canta is a Dutch four-wheeled microcar that has been in production since the late 1980s, and its short stubbiness is the result of form following function. Its tall yet extremely slender shape is ideally suited to accommodating a single, wheelchair-bound owner user, who can enter through a wide door at the rear, or alternatively, two side-doors can allow two people to travel in rather cramped and intimate conditions.

Powered by a twin-cylinder engine, its unusual-looking glassfibre body is mounted on a steel frame. The car is built at the rate of a few hundred each year.

# Zundapp Janus

Zundapp was a German firm more usually associated with motorcycle design, but in 1956 it built the Dornier Delta under licence, which was renamed the Janus. This was a most weird machine, having a door at either end resembling a sort of 'double Isetta' bubblecar with the rear passengers facing backwards in a most anti-social position, this being the reason for choosing the name Janus, who was the Roman god who faced both ways at once.

Its 250cc engine was installed between both rows of seats, as there was nowhere else to place it. Something else which had nowhere to go courtesy of this bizarre design, was any luggage – a handicap that cannot have helped endear this motoring misfit to potential customers, and it therefore comes as no surprise that the Janus was a poor seller.

# Roads are for the unadventurous

# Aerocar

While most people would agree that the car has largely been a liberating influence on our lives, for some, it could be, well, so much more so if only it could fly as well. One such dreamer was Molt Taylor from Longview, Washington, who built his first Aerocar prototype in 1948.

Finally certified for flight a full eight years later, the basic concept featured a two-seater coupé which, when on the ground, would tow behind it in a trailer all that was needed to convert itself into a plane. When flight was desired, the wings were attached and it would soon be ready for take-off. Once airborne, it could reach 125mph, but a rather more sedate 56mph was all that was possible on the ground.

After initial widespread interest resulting in Taylor taking over 200 orders, people slowly came back down to earth, realising that it was not a particularly good car or plane, and in the end, a total of five was built.

# Africar

The Africar was designed by Tony Howarth, whose idea was to build a car suited to the poor and often non-existent African roads and which could be built locally. He constructed three cars with chassis and bodywork made of wood using Citroën 2CV engines and gearboxes, Citroën GS suspension, and a variety of components from other manufacturers.

Howarth received government help and opened a factory in Lancaster in 1986. No cars ever reached customers however, and the company was dissolved in 1988, with Howarth subsequently spending time in prison for fraud.

Roads are for the unadventurous

# Amphicar

Most people are content with road-going cars, while for those who are more adventurous, there is always a 4x4 off-roader. But for some people, adventure means going really off-road and into the water, and for such people in the swinging 1960s, there was the Amphicar designed by Hans Trippel and built in Germany.

Powered by a Triumph Herald engine, it could achieve 65mph on the road, but when afloat, two propellers gave it a speed of 6mph (5.2 knots). The biggest shortcoming of the Amphicar, however, was the idiotic decision to use sheet steel for bodywork that would spend time immersed in water and rust was the enemy that sank the cars and thus eventually, the company.

# BMC Twin-engined Mini Moke

While Alec Issigonis was designing the Mini, he was simultaneously planning the Moke, aimed at military customers. Launched in 1964 and costing just £335, it came with a driver's seat, a hood, a single wiper blade, and only one colour: Spruce Green. Options included the second wiper, the remainder of the seats, heater and side screens.

A four-wheel drive version, with two engines, one fore and one aft, each driving a pair of wheels was devised, but the Army, a potential bulk purchaser, was not convinced and the project was soon dropped, even after good reactions from the press.

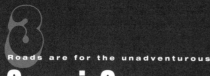

# ConvairCar

Theodore P. Hall dreamt of, and then went and built the ConvairCar in San Diego, California, helped by one of the 20th century's great car designers, Henry Dreyfuss.

The car was a glassfibre machine which weighed just 725lb, and was a pleasing design which, on terra firma, gave 45mpg. Wings, engine and a propeller could be fitted at an airfield, and then the whole ensemble was ready for flight. And fly it did, on 17 November 1947, for over an hour. Just a few days later, however, at the end of a subsequent flight, it crash-landed, and with it all hopes of any meaningful future disappeared.

# Dutton 4wd Commander

Briton Tim Dutton has been in the kit-car business for many years, but probably his most inventive design to date has been the four-wheel-drive Commander. As his website points out, there is little point making an amphibious car if it can't get out of the water because of insufficient grip, hence the sensible adoption of four-wheel drive.

Powered by either a 1,300cc Suzuki petrol engine or a 1,900cc Renault diesel, the hull is made of glassfibre, and when afloat, is capable of 6mph – the same speed in the water as the Amphicar. One crossed the English Channel in Force 4 winds to prove its seaworthiness.

# Ferves Ranger

The Ferves Ranger was built in Turin and was a most unusual looking off-road vehicle, endowed with an 18bhp Fiat 500 engine placed at the rear, which drove all four wheels. In spite of its extreme compactness, it was capable of carrying four adults, although when off road, and with such a short wheelbase, it must have been an extremely bouncy and unpleasant ride.

First shown to the public at the 1966 Turin Motor Show, the company remained in business, producing the little all-terrain oddball for five years.

# Fiat Panda 4x4

Following on from the huge success of the Audi Quattro, both in motorsport and the showrooms, every manufacturer decided in the 1980s that they needed a piece of the 4x4 action, some having more success than others.

Probably the most unlikely candidate for this treatment was the frail little Fiat Panda, but Fiat wanted a 4x4, so Steyr Puch was brought in to perform the necessary alterations. Apart from giving drive to the rear wheels as well as the front, the body was raised, and bigger tyres were fitted.

All this may have just passed as sheer comedy, had it not been for *Motor* magazine's roadtesters, who in a moment of brutality seldom equalled, managed to achieve the fastest 0–30mph time ever recorded on any car by the magazine, by revving the 1-litre engine up to its red line, and with second gear selected, dumping the clutch. The car's lightness gave little inertia, and it leapt to 30mph virtually instantaneously. After that, the fun was over, but for one glorious moment, the weird little machine was bathed in unexpected glory.

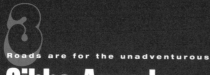

# Gibbs Aquada

There have been numerous amphibious designs over the decades, but none has come close to the Gibbs Aquada in terms of either performance or cost.

Launched in 2003 at a price of £150,000, this was no cheap car or boat, but it combined the best of both worlds, coming equipped with a 2.5-litre V6 engine installed in a glassfibre bodyshell that was fitted to a bonded aluminium space-frame chassis. It could reach 100mph on land and over 30mph (26 knots) on water. Once afloat, the wheels retracted into the bodywork at the touch of a button, converting it into a proper boat whose low centre of gravity ensured it would not capsize.

# Glenfrome Profile

The Range Rover has always been a superbly competent off-roader, but for some who may be impressed by its performance, the shape was maybe just a little conservative. Step forward Glenfrome, a Bristol-based company who had previously turned Triumph Dolomite Sprints into mid-engined sports cars. They employed the services of ex-Marcos stylist Dennis Adams to transform the worthy mud-plugger into something appealing to wealthy, mainly Middle-East clients.

The result, unveiled to the world on 17 October 1985 at the London Motorfair, Earls Court, was a bizarre-looking, high-up two-door sports car called the Profile, with a starting price tag the wrong side of £50,000. Very few were sold, and the company folded a year later.

# Herzog Conte

The 1979 Herzog Conte, as the components specialist might be able to spot, was made with a large number of Ford parts screwed, riveted and welded into a steel hull (Mk1 Granada grille, anyone?). Graced with a both low- and high-ratio gearbox, it was capable of nearly 100mph on tarmac, while clever use of its two propellers would allow more manoeuvrability in the water than most amphibious cars could hope for. Predictably, few were made.

# Lamborghini LM002

The story behind the Lamborghini company is intriguing inasmuch as Ferruccio Lamborghini, a wealthy Italian industrialist who made tractors and air-conditioning equipment, became disillusioned with his Ferrari and vowed to build something better, and set about producing some of the world's finest sports cars, and the world's first supercar, the Miura.

Quite what made Lamborghini attack the 4x4 market is not recorded, but the LM002 from 1982 was the result of that decision, and at over 16ft in length, it was a real monster, complete with a 7-litre 450bhp V12 engine. It was capable of 126mph, reaching 60mph from standstill in 8.5 seconds, but its fuel consumption of just 7mpg was shameful.

The deft hand that had previously designed the Miura and Countach, however, seems to have been on holiday when the LM002 was being drawn. The American military reputedly looked at using it, but finding it lacking in certain areas, used it as the inspiration for their own, home-grown version, the Hummer.

Roads are for the unadventurous

# Rapport Excelsior

The Range Rover has always had wealthy admirers who want to personalise the car. The late 1970s Rapport Excelsior, however, took this dubious art-form to an entirely different level building the 'only off-road limousine in the world'.

There were various questions a Rapport client would have to ask himself, such as: how many wheels do I need? Or, how many doors do I want? Or how many seats should I have, and how many electro-hydraulic hunting seats sticking out of the roof will be necessary? Also, what material or hide do I want my seats covered in? Even the front of the car was not left untouched and a mock Rolls-Royce radiator grille was available.

# Rinspeed Splash

Cars and water are not natural companions, but many designers and inventive minds have tried to marry them, with varying degrees of success. The 2004 Rinspeed Splash from Switzerland was different, however, as it transformed not from a car into a boat, but into a hydrofoil, soaring over the water with the ultra-lightweight carbon-fibre body lifted clear of the surface. This was achieved by a clever system of panels, including the rear spoiler, which rotated through 180° to form the rear hydrofoil, while the front hydrofoils emerged from either sill behind the front wheels.

It was capable of a highly respectable 52mph (45 knots) on the water, but when on the road, it had the looks of a highly desirable sports car. Powered by an ecologically sound natural gas-fuelled engine, it could propel its occupants to 62mph in just 5.9 seconds, and on to a top speed of 140mph.

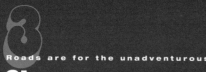

# Skycar

The Skycar is the brainchild and life's work of Californian multi-millionaire Dr Paul Moller. Joining the surprisingly large number of people who have tried to leave the traffic jams behind, or perhaps more accurately below, Moller has so far succeeded in getting early prototypes hovering above astounded spectators, and the next step with the Skycar is to get it not just hovering, but capable of controlled forward flight.

He predicts this is imminently possible, and that once fully operational, it will hopefully fly at 350mph, cruising at 29,000 feet while returning 28mpg.

# The Amphibus

Dotted around the world are people who, having had an unusual dream, then go ahead and turn the vision into a car. Nick Topping was one such Briton, who, starting in 1994, built his machine in little over a year using a steel hull, an aluminium shed, a Ford Transit diesel engine, a gearbox from a Land Rover and wheels from a Fiat van. The end result was a totally unique amphibian camper van capable of accommodating four people, and travelling at 70mph on terra firma and six knots afloat.

So confident was he of his creation's abilities, that even though he could not swim, he successfully crossed the Solent from the UK mainland to the Isle of Wight.

Roads are for the unadventurous

# WaterCar

With a few exceptions, amphibious vehicles are slow on land and even slower in the water, with the majority having equally clumsy handling and design.

The American designed and built WaterCar, however, is different. Styled on GM's Chevrolet Camaro, it is capable of 125mph on land, and once afloat and with its wheels withdrawn into its now sleek hull, akin to the Lotus featured in the James Bond film *The Spy Who Loved Me*, it is capable of 45mph (39 knots), quite sufficient to take people water-skiing. This could rightly be described as one of the most exciting and competent leisure vehicles yet designed.

# How many wheels does a car need?

# AC Petite

Launched in 1952 as the car 'made a little better than it need be', the British AC Petite, was a three-wheeler powered by a 346cc Villiers twin motorcycle engine, giving it a cruising speed of 30mph. It cost just £330, had three forward gears and a reverse, a 12-volt electric system, full-size dipping headlamps, a tail lamp with stop light, and a hydraulic brake system.

AC claimed it was 'cheaper to run than travelling by bus or train', costing less than 1½d per mile.

# Berkeley Three-wheeler

Many post-war three-wheelers were pretty basic machines, but Berkeley cars from Bedfordshire had a reputation for quality. These were designed in 1956 by Laurie Bond, a designer never afraid of flouting conventions. His design had a glassfibre body, which was rakish and exciting, and looked like a proper car, especially from the front. Its 328cc Excelsior engine was air-cooled and drove the front wheels, making it highly successful in a variety of motor sports.

However, once the Austin-Healey Sprite arrived in 1958, most people chose it over the Berkeley and shortly afterwards, the company ceased trading, after just five short years.

# BSA Ladybird

In 1960, bubblecars were still enjoying great popularity, and the Birmingham-based BSA motorcycle company decided to build its own version to follow this trend. Using the engine, gearbox and rear suspension of the BSA Sunbeam/Triumph Tigress scooter mated to a chassis and frame of steel tubing, a prototype painted bright red was built. Its bodywork, however, formed from hand-beaten steel, proved too complex for mass-production so a new design was called for. This was no easy task, and took two years to develop, by which time the bubblecar craze had passed. Happily, the original prototype still exists.

# Carver

In the 21st century, the age of the three-wheeler, it would appear, is still not over, if the Carver from Holland is anything to go by.

This thoroughly modern machine offers all sorts of thrills virtually no previous three-wheeler has been able to. However, apart from being exceptionally well built and luxuriously appointed (how does a leather and alcantara-trimmed interior sound?), its chief party trick is being able to tilt into corners in the manner of a motorcycle, or as its manufacturers would prefer you to think, like an aeroplane.

This luxury does not come cheap, however, and it seems destined to remain a plaything for high days and holidays rather than everyday transport, with its high-tech fun appeal.

# Commuter Triton

The 1979 Commuter Triton from Florida was a development of the Seabring Vanguard, and was an electric two-seater oddity of truly hideous appearance which somehow made it into (very limited) production at the end of the 1970s. It looked very much like an advert designed to scare kids of what might happen to their powers of imagination if they took drugs. It had a range of 50 miles at a speed of 35mph.

# Cursor

The Cursor was a weird little three-wheeler designed in 1985 by Alan Hatswell and built by Replicar Ltd of Kent, who normally produced replica kit cars, principally of Jaguars and Bugattis.

Powered by a 49cc moped engine and seating only one person, it was aimed at 16-year-olds in the UK who were not allowed to drive a proper car for another year. Because of legal restrictions, it was unable to exceed 30mph, but the upside of this was a fuel consumption figure in the region of 90mpg. Costing £1,724, it only sold in penny numbers between 1985 and 1987.

# David

The David three-wheeler microcar was built in the early 1950s in Spain, and looked very much like a fairground dodgem car. It was powered by a 345cc 10bhp air-cooled motorcycle engine which was fixed to the front wheel assembly so that it turned with the wheel.

Its bodywork was made from sheet steel and was attached to a tubular steel chassis. The weird little two-seater had a top speed of 50mph. Of the estimated 75 examples that were built, there are several survivors.

Built in 1952 in Totnes, Devon, the EEC Workers' Playtime took its name from the popular BBC Radio programme.

It is not clear what persuaded the company to build such a car, or to style it on a squashed caravan, but the guilt for this latter act falls upon the equally unlikely named Richard 'Dick' Turpin. Pushing the car along at a cruising speed of 37mph was a 250cc Excelsior motorcycle engine.

No Workers' Playtimes were ever sold. It may be that the design was not sufficiently appealing, but the choice of name can hardly have attracted potential customers.

# Felber Autoroller

The Autoroller was designed by Ernst Marold in Vienna and was shown as a prototype in 1950, a full two years before it went into production. History may judge that time to have been wasted, as the appearance of the dumpy little three-wheeler was not improved during this period. Looking not unlike a Messerschmitt, but without its cuteness or correctness of proportion, it had a 400cc 15bhp air-cooled engine at the rear that drove the rear wheel.

In total, about 400 examples were sold in two years of production, less than 5 per cent of the sales total of the vastly superior Messerschmitt.

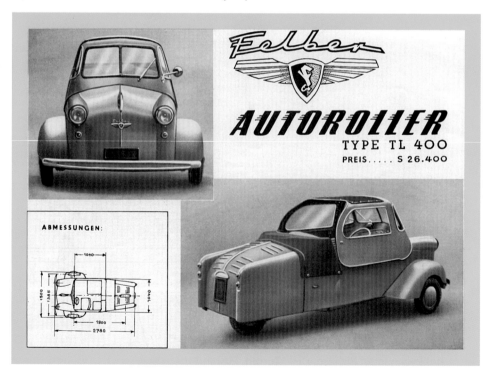

# Gaia Deltoid

The Gaia Deltoid was an interesting kit car from Hampshire launched in 1996. Its running gear comprised of most parts of a motorcycle (everything, in fact, apart from the front wheel, forks and handlebars), and interestingly, the bike could subsequently be retrieved from the machine if its owner had second thoughts. Designed to take the running gear from a range of different bikes, the power and performance obviously varied dramatically, spanning from 65bhp to 175bhp. At launch, the demonstrator was built using a Suzuki GSXR-1100, thereby justifying its claim to be 'One wheel short of a Supercar.'

# Gordon

Labelled 'Britain's Finest Three-wheeler Family Car' it was in all probability the firm's marketing department that awarded this title to the 1954-built machine from Bidston, Cheshire. The Gordon's 8bhp Villiers 197cc motorcycle engine was perched just a few inches below the driver's right elbow, and to help it along, it had three forward gears, plus reverse, giving it a top speed of 45mph.

Less than 10ft long, the Gordon was allegedly capable of carrying two adults and two children 'in big car comfort'. It was simplicity itself, especially the weatherproofing, where a folding hood and plastic clip-on side screens were all there was to stop the owner wishing they had taken the bus instead.

# Grinnall Scorpion

'Driving the Scorpion to the full, you're simply unable to stop yourself from smiling', boasts Grinnall's publicity material. Its sleek shape hints at the performance available, and a quick glance at the technical specifications confirms beyond doubt the full potential of this weird car.

Built in Bewdley, Worcestershire, the fastest Scorpion comes with the 1,100cc four-cylinder 16-valve DOHC BMW motorcycle engine delivering 125bhp, with a top speed of 'approx. 130mph', and of dispatching the sprint from standstill to 60mph in 4.5 seconds. While its looks are unconventional, Grinnall's Scorpion is a true performance machine, able to match most four-wheeled sports cars.

# Isetta Pickup

The Isetta was the car that gave birth to the name 'bubblecar'. Designed and built initially in Italy, and later under licence in both Germany and Brighton by BMW, this symbol of the late 1950s was powered by either a 247cc or 297cc motorcycle unit. It could carry up to three people, all of whom gained access through the large door at the front. There were stories of car-park attendants in London, where cars were parked nose to tail for space efficiency reasons, becoming trapped in them as certain models did not have a reverse gear and so once driven up close to the car in front, the occupant was unable to get out.

Most weird of all, however, was the simple addition of a very small open or enclosed cargo area to the rear of the car, which turned the strange machine into a truly bizarre vehicle, of sorts or a larger cargo area with two rear wheels fitted to a truncated Isetta front, turning it into the pickup seen here on show at the Bruce Weiner Microcar Museum.

# Jephcott Micro

The British-built Jephcott Micro was launched in 1987, and was a development of the Jephcott Tilting Trike of 1980. This had been partially enclosed and was powered by a 75cc two-stroke engine giving 100mpg. Its younger brother, the Micro, was a handsome three-wheeler that was clothed in a clean, elegant and fully enclosed body, seating its passengers one behind the other. It was significantly more advanced than the Trike in many ways, including an engine of 350cc, and its automatic tilting mechanism was now operated by hydraulics, with a maximum tilt angle of 25°.

# Martin Stationette

'If at first you don't succeed...' must have been one of the mottos learnt early in the life of James V. Martin, inventor of the Martin Aerodynamic (featured elsewhere in this book), the Martin Martinette and this, his last attempt; the Martin Stationette from 1950. Its strange body was built on an all-wooden monocoque frame, and the diminutive car was designed with the aim of reducing urban congestion. It had three forward gears, and a top speed of 60mph – a speed at which it must have been quite scary. It was marketed at the 1954 World Motor Sports Show as 'America's economy car of the future'. But its biggest problem, looks apart, was that by then cars in America were busy getting bigger and more flamboyant, and people didn't bother much with funny-looking economy cars. Perhaps none too surprisingly, it failed to attract any investors or buyers, and this, the only example ever built, is now on display at the Lane Motor Museum in Nashville, Tennessee, along with its sister, the equally unlikely Aerodynamic.

The 1953 Meyra 200 was the second design from this German company, and was weird by any standard.

It was a three-wheeler, with its single rear wheel powered by a 197cc Ilo single-cylinder engine. Its front end was an unusual shape, with half of it opening to provide access for the car's occupants, although the relatively small aperture made it difficult for all but the slight of figure to get in or out. In total, a little over 500 were built.

# Morgan M3W

Looking at the Morgan M3W, it would be easy to assume that this is a lovely 1930s piece of budget motoring, and to an extent, you'd be right. But, although the car was originally designed and sold back in the days before television, it has now, in the second decade of the 21st century, been reinvigorated and launched back on sale. Among its concessions to modernity are better tyres and brakes, a five-speed gearbox from Mazda (complete with reverse gear), and a fuel-injected V-Twin engine from Harley Davidson, capable of delivering huge numbers of smiles per gallon. Everything else is there to provide the modern motorist with the 'this is what Granddad must have felt like' experience.

# Mumford Musketeer

The Musketeer was designed and built in the mid-1970s by Brian Mumford in Gloucester in penny numbers over a number of years and was offered as a kit. It was, however, a better kit than many, and featured an aluminium alloy monocoque chassis, an aerodynamic shape with flat underside and concealed headlamps. The mechanicals, however, came from the rather less inspiring Vauxhall Viva HA, which while it meant there was a plentiful supply of spares, somewhat dampened any interest in an otherwise potentially plausible car.

# Nobel 200

'Travel in style for half a penny a mile', was how the strange-looking Nobel was sold. Built in London between 1959 and 1962, it was an anglicised Fuldamobil design from Germany, built under licence. Capable of carrying four adults, it was available as either a three-wheeler or a curious four-wheeler, with the rear two wheels sited closely together, and it came with a Sachs 200cc two-stroke engine placed behind the rear passengers.

Costing just £135 new, its fuel consumption of nearly 90mpg led its manufacturers to claim, it 'makes motoring almost as cheap as breathing.'

From the only car company ever to produce cars commercially on the Isle of Man, and weighing in at just 130lb, the tiny glassfibre Peel from 1962 cost less than £200 when new. It could be driven by a 16-year-old without a full licence as it only had a 49cc DKW moped engine to push it along. It had three forward gears and no reverse, so to turn it round, the driver had to get out, walk around to the back of the car, and pick up the rear by the thoughtfully provided chrome handle, to reposition it in the required direction: simplicity itself.

# Purves Dynasphere

'Who says cars have to have four wheels?' Dr John Purves, following designs originally drawn by Leonardo da Vinci, came up with the Dynasphere in the early 1930s, which he demonstrated at Brooklands and on the beach at Weston-super-Mare. On one occasion, he achieved 25mph, which does not sound too scary until the need to brake or steer arises, and the inability to perform either proved its downfall. The result of trying to brake with anything other than the meekest of pressure was a phenomenon known as 'gerbiling', where the rider would simply stop sitting at the bottom of the wheel, and become part of it, rotating as it carried on virtually oblivious to the attempts to stop it.

This did not dissuade the good doctor, however, pictured here demonstrating his wonderful machine at Brooklands. He was even photographed in 1932 with a model of a fully-enclosed passenger-carrying Dynasphere, although this was never built.

# Scott Sociable

The First World War introduced many people to motoring, and once demobbed, many were not willing to return simply to walking, cycling or public transport. The Scott Sociable was a machine with its roots in the latter days of the war, when it had been designed by Alfred Angas Scott as a gun car, and in peacetime, its manufacturers hoped to find customers amongst those who wanted to drive but could not afford a conventional car.

Powered by Scott's two-stroke 587cc engine, it looked curiously unbalanced, and its unusual arrangement of wheels made unwise any attempt at the higher speeds it was capable of, as neither steadiness nor controllability was guaranteed. A little over 100 Sociables were made.

# Stimson Scorcher

Barry Stimson launched the Scorcher in the long hot summer of 1976, and it looked considerably less mundane than its Mini front subframe origins might have suggested it should. It could seat three, including the driver, and after some head scratching among the licensing authorities, it was classified as a motorcycle and sidecar combination.

Available as a kit that could be carried home on the roof of another car, it used the entire front subframe of BL's Mini for its engine, steering and front suspension. The main frame was made from steel, and was clothed in a single piece of glassfibre. Once built, the machine was capable of a frightening top speed of 100mph, while it cost only £385 to buy. Only 30 Scorchers were ever built, although happily, a number still exist.

The 1983 Trihawk, as the name suggests, was an American-built three-wheeler that used the 1,299cc four-cylinder boxer engine, transmission and front-wheel drive layout from a Citroën GSA, a car never sold in the USA. With its front suspension and the rear wheel trailing arm from a Renault 5, there was a real French flavour to the car, although its rakish, two-seater glassfibre bodywork hid these humble origins well, and when *Road & Track* magazine tested one, proclaimed it to be one of the best cornering vehicles they had ever driven, a result of its incredibly low centre of gravity.

# Trojan

The Trojan was an anglicised version of the Heinkel bubblecar, available from 1960 until 1965, boasting an extremely appealing 95mpg from its 200cc engine. It was capable of cruising at 55mph while transporting, according to the sales brochure, 'two adults and two children in luxury', as well as 'gloves, handbags, maps, cameras and the kiddies' bits and pieces.' The brochure also claimed it would 'cruise along smartly and comfortably at the rate of 20 miles per shilling!' Being so small, it was ideal for parking in towns, and on sunny days its occupants could peel back the fabric sunroof for extra fun.

# Tuscan Gyro X

The Tuscan Gyro X is surrounded in mystery, but there is sufficient evidence to believe that it really did exist, even if it subsequently vanished without trace.

It was built in 1967 in Northbridge, California by Gyro Transport Services, and the supremely aerodynamic styling was the work of Alex Tremulis, a designer of great merit who had worked on the 1933 Duesenberg, Cord and the Ford X2000 concept car before setting up as a freelance design consultant.

Apart from a sales brochure, most of the detailed description comes from a five-page article published in *Science and Mechanics* in September 1967, which included impressions of a drive in the 15ft 5in long, 47in high car. It was powered by a 1,275cc BMC engine located at the rear, which powered the front-positioned, 22in gyroscope hydraulically. This rotated at 6,000rpm and generated 1,300lb ft of torque, which apparently kept the whole car absolutely rock steady. Although only powered by a relatively small engine, it was allegedly capable, thanks to its streamlining and smaller number of wheels on the road, of a top speed of 125mph. The gyroscope required just 1 per cent of the available engine power once up to speed.

Conspiracy theorists claim its disappearance was linked to US government interest in the potential of gyroscope-based vehicles.

The 1961 VH was a Spanish minicar which took its name from the initials of its creator, Vargas Hernandez. Looking like a cross between a Citroën 2CV and a Messerschmitt, its single rear wheel did the driving, powered by a vertical twin two-stroke engine of Hernandez's own design.

His decision to make his own engine rather than following the conventional wisdom of buying in a readily available unit ensured the costs of putting the machine into production would always be massively too high, regardless of how good the engine might have been, and in the end, only one car was ever built.

# Wolseley Gyrocar

Is it a motorbike? Is it a car? No, it's a Wolseley Gyrocar!

Whilst many cars of 1912 were still relatively crude devices, the Gyrocar was a fiendishly complicated machine, devised by a Russian Count, Dr Peter Schilovski, and built by Wolseley in Coventry. Up front, it had a Wolseley-Vickers engine, which drove the rear wheel by means of a prop-shaft, and also powered the dynamo responsible for keeping the gyroscope in motion. This gyroscope enabled the near three-ton vehicle to remain upright regardless of lateral forces, and startled pedestrians by apparently defying the laws of nature.

The Gyrocar was a fantastic answer to a question no-one had asked, and despite its highly improbable appearance, it really worked, being capable of reversing, cornering, and performing every manoeuvre a car with more wheels could.

Only one was ever built and, infuriatingly, this was destroyed after the end of the Second World War.

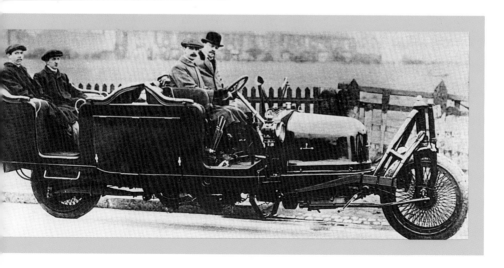

# ZAP Alias

Traditionally, two problems have dogged electric cars: the speed, or in most cases, lack of, and the distance over which they can continue to deliver it. With the ZAP Alias, so called because it's 'a car that can be anything you want it to be', according to Gary Starr, Team Leader at ZAP, it is claimed it can travel at 100mph and has a range of 100 miles. It has been developed by ZAP of California in association with Jonway Auto of China, and features solar panels to help keep its batteries topped up. It also features, however, electric windows, power steering and GPS navigation, which if used, must surely reduce the range it's capable of covering between charges.

# Think futuristic

Think futuristic

# Argonaut Smoke

Back in 1960 $26,000 was a lot of money to pay for a car, but that was the asking price for the outrageously ambitious Argonaut Smoke. Optional equipment included air-conditioning, telephone, refrigerated food and drink compartments and a trans-continental radio. The detail was phenomenal, right down to a stainless-steel 32-gallon fuel tank, honeycombed to prevent a fuel surge.

This was to be a real American supercar, but only one is known ever to have been delivered. Nevertheless, the extravagant brochure and fabulous illustrations make for interesting reading.

# Bertone BAT

The highly respected Italian design house of Bertone has, over the decades, produced some wonderful cars, and between 1953 and 1955, was responsible for a series of BAT cars. Their ultra-sleek coachwork may have made them look like extras on a Batman film set, but in reality, BAT was short for Berlinetta Aerodinamica Tecnica.

They were based on the Alfa Romeo 1900 floorpan, and were stunningly beautiful, with the BAT 7 having a highly commendable drag coefficient of just 0.19. Even today, their sleek beauty does not look especially dated, and happily, several survive in private hands.

# Bricklin SV1

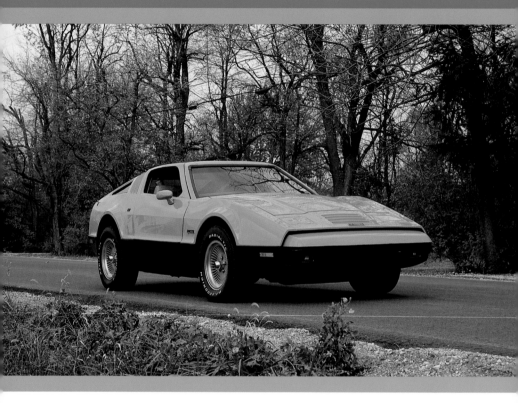

The Bricklin SV1 was designed by Malcolm Bricklin in 1974, and built in a factory paid for by the Canadian government as part of a jobs creation programme.

Although technically a sports car, and fitted with (troublesome) gull-wing doors, it was designed very much with safety in mind, with a large impact-resistant front bumper and numerous safety features throughout its interior. Budget control, however, was not a strong point with the company, perhaps due to it being bankrolled by the government, and when it was discovered after making less than 3,000 cars that each one cost twice as much to make as its selling price, the venture folded.

# Charbonneaux Ellipsis

One idea that the more 'free-thinking' car designers keep coming back to is that of placing four wheels in a diamond formation. A recent example of this is the Ellipsis, designed by Philipe Charbonneaux, an eminent French industrial designer by that time in his eighties, exhibited at the 1992 Paris Motor Show.

Principal among the alleged benefits of the wheel location was its ability to manoeuvre into small gaps and perform a U-turn in just over twice its length, while its Kevlar, spear-like shape was apparently a safety feature. Pedestrians who might, if hit by a conventional car, be thrown further on to it, when struck by the Ellipsis, would simply glance off the tapering sides. This theory, thankfully, was never put to the test, and the concept did not go any further than being exhibited at shows. Although powered by a VW Beetle engine driving the middle two wheels, it was never actually witnessed in motion.

# Chrysler Airflow

In 1934, the science of streamlining was still in its infancy, but increasingly its influence was to be seen in steam locomotives such as the world speed record breaking *Mallard*, and various aeroplanes of the period. The public perception was that streamlining suggested speed, and so Chrysler of America reasoned a car was a prime candidate for the slippery and smooth lines of this design genre.

The Airflow they launched, was indeed a radical shape, designed by Paul Jaray, and although a great leap forward in design terms, was too much too soon for the conservative car-buying public, and commercially it was a flop.

# Chrysler Turboflite

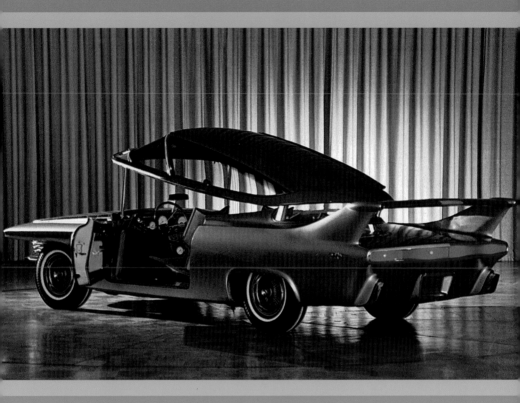

There can be few concept cars ever to have been more striking in appearance than Chrysler's 1961 Turboflite. Powered by a gas turbine engine which was half the weight of the standard V8 as fitted to most American cars, it had additional braking courtesy of a deceleration flap at the rear of the car.

None of this, however, was worthy of note compared with its *pièce de résistance*. The entire upper area of the car, which included the windscreen and roof, formed a canopy that lifted as a single piece when any door was opened, to help gain access, and lowered again once the doors were closed. Perhaps it should have been called a 'Turboflite of fancy', for here was another example of designers trying to reinvent the wheel and coming up with something which ultimately turned out to be the answer to a question no-one had been daft enough to ask.

**Think futuristic**

# Citroën Coccinelle

The Citroën Coccinelle was a startling car, whose shape was so smooth, aerodynamic and functionally right, it would be hard to date. In actual fact, it was built in 1953, from a design by Frenchman André Lefebvre.

It was front-wheel drive powered by a flat-twin engine, and was built using ultra-lightweight materials and aircraft construction techniques, resulting in a kerb weight of just 842lb. Entry was via a near full-length aircraft-style canopy, similar to that of a Messerschmitt, while devotees of modern cartoon culture might think that the view from the front shares more than a passing resemblance to Pikachu, from the *Pokemon* comics. The ultimate shame was that work was eventually stopped on the Coccinelle in favour of the much less pretty Projet C-60 in 1960.

# Citroën Projet C-60

The Projet C-60 was an attempt by Citroën designers to come up with a car to fill the gap between the 2CV and the DS at the beginning of the 1960s. Both these cars were great successes for the fiercely French and idiosyncratic company, but to paraphrase a well used cliché, desperation is the mother of mistakes, and merely blending elements of DS with Ami 6 produced what is arguably one of the least attractive cars ever to have progressed beyond the drawing board and into metal.

It offered the space and hydropneumatic suspension comfort of the DS, but came with a much smaller engine. Eventually, sense prevailed, and the project was canned.

Think futuristic

# Combidrive Mouse

The Combidrive Mouse is a three-wheeled miser that started life as an electric car in Denmark, equipped with three lead-acid batteries. Acquired by Combidrive in Wales in 1996, and fitted with a 4½hp 265cc diesel engine to power the feather-light plastic body, it entered the record books when it set the world record for the lowest ever fuel consumption, with a startling figure of 568mpg.

Weighing just 309lb, it is road legal, with lights, horn, functioning brakes, seat belts etc. and has clocked up more than 3,000 miles of commuting since its record run, with a top speed of around 40mph.

# Costin Amigo

A number of cars have used wood in various ways as part of their construction, but what makes the 1970 Costin Amigo stand out from the crowd is that its entire monocoque was made from wood. This, however, was its most interesting aspect, as its mechanicals came from the Vauxhall Victor FD. Due largely to the lightweight nature of the car, these relatively humdrum components nevertheless gave it a top speed of 137mph.

Unfortunately, startling top speeds were not enough to persuade punters to part with their cash and during its production lifetime (1970–72), a sorry total of just eight was built.

# Crossley Burney

Crossley Motors of Manchester already had 29 years' experience of building cars when, in 1934, it took on the task of building a rear-engined, highly streamlined car designed by Sir Dennistoun Burney. At 15ft 5in long, the car was enormous, and highly unorthodox right down to its engine at the rear. Inside, the car was equipped as luxuriously as possible, even to include pneumatic seat cushions beautifully clad in leather. It was, however, a heavily compromised design, which failed to deliver on many fronts. Priced at £750, approximately 20 were built, and at least one survives, owned by the National Motor Museum, Beaulieu.

# Dymaxion

The strangely named Dymaxion from 1933 was the creation of an American called Richard Buckminster Fuller, and was an extraordinarily advanced machine with two front wheels driven by a Ford V8 engine, while the single rear wheel was responsible for steering the car.

In an effort to keep the weight down, much of it was built from balsa wood and duralumin, and it was claimed to have a top speed of 120mph, while returning a fuel consumption of 40mpg. Only three were ever built, and cars number 2 and 3 were fitted with an angled periscope to help compensate for the lack of a rear window. Fortunately, the second car still survives, and is part of the collections at the National Auto Museum, Reno, Nevada.

# Edison2 VLC

The Edison2 VLC (which stands for 'very light car') is a back-to-basics approach to car design. It accepts that lightness and aerodynamics are key to real efficiencies, and so its designers have chosen a super lightweight single-cylinder 250cc engine fuelled by E85 Bio-Ethanol, rather than opting for the heavy batteries needed by electric and hybrid vehicles. Its body is made from aluminium and steel, which is cheaper and more recyclable than carbon composite materials. The savings made by this approach have shown that it only requires 5.3hp to travel at 60mph and is capable of 129mpg, with a top speed of 100mph, and a range between fill-ups of 600 miles.

Capable of seating four people, it has no electric seats or similar weight-adding features, although accepting that some luxuries are now considered essential, an iPod docking stereo system is fitted.

# Fitch Phoenix

Designed and built by ex-racing driver John Fitch in 1966, the Phoenix was perhaps inappropriately named, as only the one example, a prototype, was ever built. It was powered by a six-cylinder aluminium engine from a Corvair, and like the Porsche 911, this was rear-mounted and air-cooled, but there, any similarities between this all-American sports car and the German car end. It offered strange features including forced air-cooled seats and a tall driver's seat location, alongside more mainstream options such as a retractable roof and AM/FM radio. Capable of 130mph, it reached the first 60mph in a highly respectable 7.5 seconds. It was priced at $8,700.

A number of orders were taken for the car, but unfortunately for Fitch, Chevrolet killed off the Corvair just as the Phoenix, which relied on it for engine and other components, was ready to roll.

# Ford Gyron

Although only intended to be a concept car, the 1961 Ford Gyron was a fascinating piece of imaginative thinking combined with space-age design. With just two wheels, one at each end, the name Gyron gives away the car's main secret: its stability was to be found by employing a gyroscope. Two small outrigger wheels were positioned towards the rear of the car, and were to be deployed when ever the gyroscope was not powered up.

Further blue-sky thinking could be seen in the car's interior, where, in place of a steering wheel, there was a dial with separate rings for automatic speed and steering control, and this, combined with individual accelerator and brake pads on each foot bar, gave either passenger the ability to steer. Computers, still very much in their infancy in 1961, were all part of the package, providing the drivers with a wide array of information.

# Gatso

While the name Gatso today inspires mixed feelings in the minds of most modern motorists, in days gone by the same name may well have evoked laughter.

The inventor of both the roadside speed camera and the Gatso car was Maurice Gatsonides, a Dutch rally driver. His car, launched in 1948, was considerably funnier than his later invention, and came with three headlights and a perspex bubble-shaped roof fixed on top of its aluminium body which was most unorthodox, and visually unrewarding. Production scarcely made it into double figures before it ceased.

GATSO TYPE „4000"

# General Motors Firebird XP21

The General Motors Firebird XP21 was a product not just of its time, but more importantly, of Harley Earl, the great American designer of the 1950s, whose later cars would become icons. At the beginning of the 1950s, as the Cold War gathered pace, designing a car that looked like a jet fighter, and which was powered by a gas turbine engine, sent out a none-too-subtle propaganda message to America's foes.

There was much more to this car, however, than mere military posturing. It was a genuine attempt at advancing car design, and featured a number of systems for trialing, such as a hands-free auto-pilot which was operated by the car following a wire hidden in the surface of the test track. Two further Firebirds were developed, each more Jetson-esque than the previous.

# Ghia Selene I

The Ghia Selene I from 1959 was a truly baffling machine to look at, and one should surely be thankful that it never went beyond the concept stage. Even determining which is the front end when looking from the side was not an easy task. Once this was achieved, the car was capable of carrying six adults, with two up front, and the other four arranged in pairs facing inwards, presumably seeking moral support from each other in order to endure the mirth directed at them by pedestrians.

Peace up-front might also be short-lived, as the ability to move the steering wheel and controls from side to side could lead to disputes erupting as to who should drive. Having never been fitted with an engine, this bizarre creation would certainly have got people thinking, although perhaps not in the manner its designers had hoped for.

# Ghia Selene II

The 1962 Ghia Selene II was a fabulous design, reaching forwards to a bright future, where anything would be possible, and scientists would be working for all our benefit. Capable of seating three, the driver sat in a leather-trimmed bucket seat in the middle, steering with aircraft-style controls, while the two passengers sat either side of him in bucket seats, facing the wrong way and watching a television screen (probably still black and white).

When this amazing machine came to auction in June 2002, it realised a not-too-surprising high price of $88,125.

# Hewson Rocket

The startling Hewson Rocket is all that remains of an immediate post-war American dream. The big idea was to build an ultra-sleek, ultra-modern car and sell it for $1,000. The designing and building went well, although to modern eyes it looks more blobby than sleek. Fitted with a Ford V8, it was good for 90mph, and its aluminium body had no external protrusions at all – even the door handles were hidden. The cost of building it did not go well either: the company ran out of funds, owing $16,000 at a time when that was considered a lot of money. This example from 1946 was the only one ever built, and is now on display at the Lane Motor Museum in Nashville Tennessee.

Think futuristic

# Honda Personal Neo

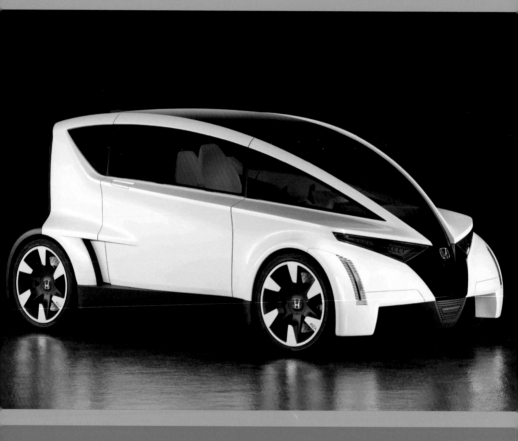

Dreaming up meaningful new names for exciting cars is something of a headache for manufacturers. Honda demonstrates the point well with this – their Personal-Neo Urban Transport, shortened to P-NUT, a concept car first shown to the public at the 2009 Los Angeles Motor Show. Seating three, the driver was centrally positioned, which gave the passengers seated behind and to each side unrivalled legroom in what was a very small car. Projected up onto the lower areas of the windscreen was a head-up display showing sat-nav information and images from the reversing camera. Although a promising and appealing design, to date Honda has shown no intention of putting it into production.

# Ikenga

The British-built Ikenga, launched in October 1968, stood just 3ft 2in high, had a 5.2-litre Chevrolet V8 engine under its beautifully hand-rolled aluminium body, and a claimed top speed of around 162mph.

The Mk1 version was styled, in the words of its creator, as 'a contemporary African mask on wheels that faced skyward to spirit.' The Mk2 version had a custom leather interior, Gucci fitted luggage, a fold-away steering wheel, fluorescent night-time driving lights, and phosphor luminescent roof panels for interior lighting. The Mk3 version, the final development, featured superbly smooth bodywork, the whole front of which hinged forwards to allow entry to the car. Other gadgets included a rear-view TV camera, an innovative accident warning system, and ultra-sound proximity sensors to aid the driver with parking.

The price tag of £9,000 killed off any hope of production.

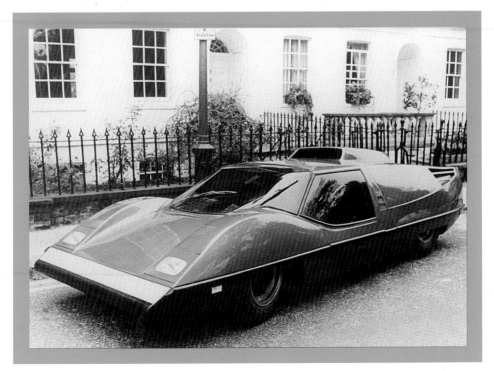

# Kaiser

During the mid-1930s, the art of streamlining proliferated in planes, trains, and in a few adventurous car designs. Perhaps none was more adventurous than the Kaiser three-wheeler from Oschersleben, Germany, launched in 1935.

This was a single-seater, with streamlining over both front wheels and the nose taken to the extreme. Its rear wheel did the driving, powered by a variety of NSU engines from 200cc to 600cc, the largest giving the missile-like car a highly creditable top speed of 75mph. The cost of production, however, made them prohibitively expensive, and very few were ever sold.

# Mallalieu Microdot

Mallalieu Engineering Ltd of Abingdon, Oxfordshire had been in existence for several years, converting MkVI Bentleys into open sports cars when Noel Hodson joined the firm. He started work on a William Towns designed microcar with a difference: this was the world's first petrol/electric hybrid, nearly 20 years ahead of Toyota's Prius.

Based on Mini subframes, it was small but was fitted out very luxuriously, and sporting its hybrid power source, the accountants worked out that to build it commercially would cost approximately £10,000 a piece, and so work stopped in 1980 after just two prototypes had been constructed.

# Marathon Corsaire

The Marathon Corsaire was a weird-looking machine originally penned by Hans Trippel, and refined by French rally driver Bernard Denis in 1953. Clothed in a lightweight glassfibre body, the 42bhp rear-mounted 850cc twin-carburettor Panhard engine gave the sort of performance one would hope for from a car developed and endorsed by a rally driver.

Performance alone, however, does not a good car make, and its unusual appearance must surely have played a part in its sorry sales total of just 17 examples.

# Minissima

William Towns (of Aston Martin Lagonda et al fame) was responsible for designing the Minissima of 1973. This clean, single-box shape, with a single door placed at the rear, was short enough to park endways on into a parking space. It used as its basis the engine and sub-frames from BL's Issigonis-styled Mini, and consequently, had no real vices, but the BL management lacked the vision to turn the Minissima from a design study into a production reality. Subsequently, the bicycle manufacturer Elswick adopted the design, renaming it the Envoy, and marketed it for a short while as a vehicle that a wheelchair-bound owner could use with great ease.

# Naro

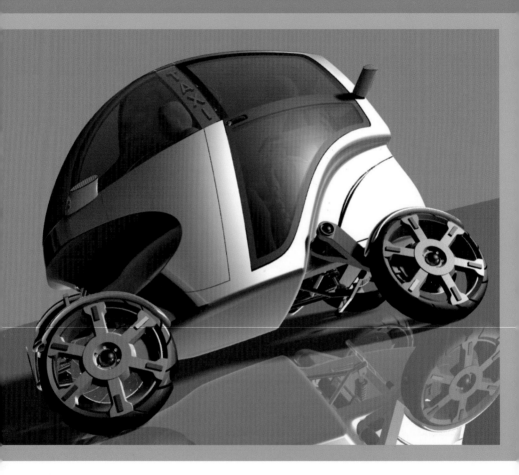

Making cars economical, or even eco-buddy, is no longer enough it would seem. To attract attention, they must, at concept stage at least, have some other attribute. The Naro, designed at Coventry University, was frugal (100mpg was the aim from a 400cc single-cylinder engine delivering 20bhp), and certainly it was striking to look at, but its party piece had to be the handling characteristics of a motorcycle, achieved by enabling it to lean its way around corners. It was not the first car to do this, but this had to be among the more avant-garde in appearance.

# Phantom Corsair

No book on weird cars would be complete without mention of the Phantom Corsair, which was the work of American Rust Heinz, the second son of H. J. Heinz, of baked beans fame.

Designed in 1937, and still looking surprisingly fresh today, it was ultra modern, and featured such gadgets as electrically opening doors. It appeared in the film *Young at Heart*, and Heinz planned to market the sleek beauty, powered by Lycoming V8 engine (as used in the Cord 810), for $14,000, but his death in a car crash in 1939 put an end to the project.

# Pininfarina Modulo

To give the 1970 Modulo its full title, it was the Pininfarina 512S Modulo design research prototype, but that seems curiously to rob it of some of its magic and majesty. Based on a Ferrari 512S, the essential wedge-shape was hugely simple, and yet the end result was staggering and captivatingly beautiful. It was enormously wide, encompassing both front and rear wheels, but its party-piece was the way the whole canopy lifted and slid forwards to let in the occupants. In reality, it may not be the easiest of cars to drive, being so wide, and with its extremities hidden from the driver's view, but as a flight of fancy, there are few designs to equal it.

The Probe 15 was stunningly sleek, standing just 29in from the ground at its highest point, and it had all the appearance of a 200mph supercar. In reality, however, performance was much more modest – its engine was from the Hillman Imp, giving a top speed of just 80mph.

Due to its extremely low profile, it was not possible to equip it with doors, and entry was effected through the sunroof. Unveiled at the 1969 Racing Car Show, and priced at £950, it was greeted with rapturous praise subsequently from the press. Only one was ever sold, however.

# SAIC Ye Zi Leaf concept car

Thinking 'outside the box' is something every concept car designer aims to do, to predict the future. Those responsible for the Shanghai Automotive Ye Zi concept appear to have taken a more fundamental approach, however, by asking 'what box?' In leaving behind almost every idea ever incorporated in a car – apart from giving it four wheels equally shared between two axles – the Ye Zi's creators have produced not only a startlingly elegant machine, but one full of novel ideas, some of which are more likely to work than others. Its leaf-shaped roof contains photovoltaic electricity generating cells, and its hubcaps are turbines that generate electricity whilst the car is in motion. They claim it runs on renewable energy and actually emits oxygen, which makes it the world's first carbon-negative car.

The Skyline X-50 was another ambitious American attempt from the early 1950s to build a car for tomorrow. The product of aviation company Skyline Inc., the designers tried to bring to the car some of their aviation experience. Apart from the sleek (for its day) styling, the main feature worthy of note was the banishing of controls from the dashboard, and relocating them in an 'aircraft-type control quadrant'. This was located between the front seats and used levers to control the throttle, mixture, electric overdrive disconnect, spark control and lights. It was aimed to sell the car for less than $3,000, but tellingly, at the bottom of the sales brochure, it reads: 'A dream?... You said it!' None was ever sold.

# Volkswagen XL1

The Volkswagen XL1 is a hybrid that shows saving the planet doesn't have to involve driving dull vehicles with no style and even less performance. Its top speed is limited to 99mph; it can reach 62mph in less than 12 seconds; and it can make a gallon of standard diesel fuel last a staggering 313 miles. Its stylish body is made from carbon reinforced plastic resin, its wheels from lightweight magnesium, and the brake discs are ceramic, all of which contribute to a total weight of just 795kg. Unfortunately, it is only a concept car, albeit a fully functioning one, but its designers claim future cars will adopt much of what we see here.

# Cheap, but not always cheerful

Cheap, but not always cheerful

# American Microcar

The American Microcar only survived for two years, which is perhaps not in itself surprising in a country where space has never been an issue and there is no great history of making small cars.

Launched in 1979 and looking more suited to the streets of Bombay than America, it was available either with a 49cc moped engine or an electric motor. It was a crude device, in essence a three-wheeled chassis with roll-cage and windscreen, on which the purchaser could choose to specify a roof and side panels at extra cost.

The Auto-Cub, built in America in 1956, was a machine which most people would probably never have dared to try to sell, being so crude, basic and home-built in appearance. Its single-seater body was made from plywood, looked like a horribly cheap DIY kit, and housed a 1.6hp Briggs & Stratton engine behind the driver, who steered the pointless machine with a tiller, at speeds of up to 15mph. There were no lights, windscreen, doors or even padding on the seat, just somewhere to sit and feel very vulnerable and foolish. Few sold, even at the low price of $170.

# BMA Brio

There are some cars whose appearance is so weird and haphazard it appears that no effort went into the design process whatsoever. One such car was the BMA Brio, a microcar from Italy.

Launched in 1978, it seems that the Brio was from the school of thought that says if it is a microcar, the more stupid, ugly and downright bizarre the appearance, the better. It had a 47cc Sachs moped engine driving one of the rear wheels, giving miserly fuel consumption, and miserable performance.

# Briggs & Stratton

The majority of weird cars have either three or four wheels, and several have less than that, but the extremely primitive American Briggs & Stratton 'buckboard', as it was known, had five.

Looking like a soap-box Derby racer, this crude machine was available from 1919 to 1924, pushed along by Briggs & Stratton's version of a Smith Motor Wheel, which was akin to a bicycle wheel with an engine inside it, fixed to the back of the cart. When the pushing stopped, there was scant braking available.

Remarkably, they sold this scary machine, without any suspension, for $200, and it found eager buyers for a period of six years.

Cheap, but not always cheerful

# Coronet

The Coronet was another weird, late-1950s British attempt at making a full-size car at microcar prices. It was a glassfibre bodied three-wheeler with a fake radiator grille mimicking bigger cars, open-topped and capable of carrying three people.

Its single rear wheel was driven by a 328cc 18bhp Excelsior engine which was placed just in front of this wheel and behind the seats. The majority of the rest of the car's running gear came from the Standard 8.

Approximately 250 were built before its demise in 1960, hastened no doubt by the exceptional value of the Mini launched the previous year.

# Eshelman Sport Car

"An easy way to a good score!"

UP TO
36 HOLES
PER GALLON!

The Eshelman Sport Car was built by Chester L. Eshelman Co. of Baltimore, Maryland, which normally made garden tractors, but between 1953 and 1960, decided to expand their range.

The Sport Car was a bizarre machine, available in either child or adult size, and with its top speed of just 20mph from its 250cc single-cylinder engine, was best suited to only the very shortest of trips. Its garden tractor origins were easy to spot from its lack of suspension, its absence of instrumentation, an inability to charge its own battery, and most worryingly, its brakes, which consisted of rubber paddles rubbing against the tyres: two for the child's version, and four for the adult's. Starting the comedy machine was by a rope pull, while stopping it involved fumbling about in a hot engine bay trying to find the engine kill button.

It was exceptionally heavy because many of the components one might expect to have been made from sheet steel were cast – even the bodywork. Available in either red or yellow, the front and rear panels were actually the same, but the front had a cast grille attached where the rear's aperture was filled in with a piece of plywood.

Cheap, but not always cheerful

# Fairthorpe Atom

The Fairthorpe Atom is the ugly duckling car that just stayed dumpy looking and appeared curiously unfinished, with options listed including such basics as hubcaps, front bumpers and even exterior door handles.

Built in Buckinghamshire, it was only available in 1953 and was equipped with either manual starting or optional electric starter. As with so many of the cheapies of the 1950s, its principal appeal was frugality, but at least it had a full set of four wheels. Its body was described as being made of non-corrosive material, while its shopping shelves were 'of an area totalling many times more than other cars.'

# Goggomobil

Not only a weird name, the Goggomobil made by Hans Glas of Germany was bizarre to look at, and scary to drive. With its 400cc engine placed at the rear, it was capable of 60mph, at which speeds frightening amounts of oversteer made the little beast a real handful on roads with anything other than the driest of surfaces.

The car was a descendant of the Goggo scooter, first launched in 1951, and which was available with a crude electric version of pre-selector transmission. The company was acquired by BMW in 1966, and the marque disappeared two years later.

The HM Free-Way, from Burnsville, Minnesota, (HM stood for high mileage) looked as un-American as a car could: it was small, carrying only one person, was crude in appearance, and just did not possess any of the normal attributes of an American automobile. It could even be ordered with a small diesel engine rather than the usual 6hp electric motor, or a choice of two less than half-litre petrol engines.

Its glassfibre body was ugly, with only one headlight, and it looked more like a post-war European austerity car than a late 1970s US machine.

The 1974 Ranger Cub was an extraordinary beast to look at, resembling a cross between a bath tub and a boat. Built in a disused cinema in Essex, its amphibious appearance, was, however, completely coincidental, and no claim for buoyancy in water was ever made.

Available as a kit costing just £199, it used the Mini engine and front subframe attached to a space frame chassis, as well as a number of other components such as the windscreen from the donor Mini. Towards the end of its short lifespan, it was also available in four-wheeled form, and even an electrically driven prototype was developed, but not sold.

# Rodley

THE **RODLEY**

Looking not unlike the sort of vehicle a child might draw, the Rodley's production lifespan was perhaps not unexpectedly short (1954–55), and the Leeds firm's ambitious aims of producing between 50 and 60 cars per week were never realised.

Here was a car that not only looked crude, but was also incredibly unsophisticated mechanically. It boasted cable-operated brakes and chain steering and was noted for harsh and violent vibrations making the journey for any of the four people who could be crammed into its sparsely finished cabin a most horrid event. In total, approximately 65 Rodleys were built.

# Urbanina

The Urbanina was a weird design with good intentions. Designed by the Marquis Piergirolamo Bargagli and launched at the 1965 Turin Motor Show, the minuscule Urbanina measured just 6ft 4 in length, was powered by a 175cc motorcycle engine, and was aimed at reducing traffic congestion in towns.

While this was a laudable aim, it remains unanswered as to why the Marquis chose to offer some with bodywork more reminiscent of a laundry basket than a car. Other versions were also available, and later models came with a 200cc engine, or even an electric motor.

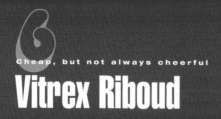

# Vitrex Riboud

The Vitrex Riboud was designed by Jacques Riboud in 1974, and was sold as another French vehicle that could be driven without a driving licence (or dignity).

Nicknamed 'le Hanneton' (the bug), it was designed as a city car, but ended up looking like a very silly car, with uncomplicated straight lines dominating the simple glassfibre bodywork. It was powered by a 47cc Sachs moped engine and was basic transport at its most simple. It must surely have been a great incentive to take a driving test as soon as possible, in order to qualify to drive other more pleasing vehicles.

# Whitwood Monocar

The Whitwood Monocar was built in Portsmouth, and was capable of carrying two people in tandem style. It could be bought with engines ranging in size from 150cc to 1 litre, and the occupants were seated in bucket seats, fitted snugly inside the plywood body which came complete with a hood.

Ranging in price from just £49 to a still-reasonable £85, the design raised much interest, but this did not, unfortunately translate into firm orders, and over the two years from 1934 to 1936 that it was on sale very few ever found buyers.

The Willam was an Italian microcar from the late 1960s designed by, and used components including engines, from Lambretta scooters, but was actually built by LAWIL. Powered by a 125cc engine, it had a four-speed gearbox, 10in wheels and drum brakes, and although fitted with windscreen wipers and headlights, which were legal requirements, there were no doors: a chain hung across the space on each side of the car where a door would usually be found.

It enjoyed more popularity than might be expected in some European countries, where it was permitted to drive such a small car without a licence.

# CHAPTER SEVEN

# We don't normally make cars like this

We don't normally make cars like this

# Allard P2 Safari Eight-seater estate

Sydney Allard was a British racing driver who became a manufacturer as a by-product of his racing. In 20 years of car manufacture at his base in London, he made less than 2,000 vehicles and these were all either sports-racing cars or performance luxury cars.

One such machine was the P2 Safari Eight-seater estate from 1953. While its external woodwork was reminiscent of the Morris 1000 Traveller, its 200bhp Cadillac V8 engine, rich carpeting, hide-covered seats and polished wood fascia and door-cappings ensured that there the similarities ended. A total of just 21 P2 saloons and estates were built in three years.

# Alvis TB14

Launched to the public at the famous 1948 Earls Court Motor Show, the sales brochures claimed the Alvis TB14 from Coventry was a 'striking combination of graceful line…' Others however, saw it as a truly ugly car. The show car (in a startling crimson with ivory leather interior) had a cocktail cabinet mounted in one of the doors, and for the ladies, a 'beauty parlour', situated in the dash.

In comparison with William Lyons's styling masterpiece, the Jaguar XK120, launched at the same show, the ugly duckling TB14 stood no chance, and only 100 examples were ever built.

# Aquila

The Aquila was the result of a competition launched at the beginning of the 1970s to build a car of the future, to be launched in 1976, yet using the very humdrum mechanicals of nobody's favourite, the Austin Maxi.

It was designed by Christopher Field of Brixham in Devon, and was exhibited at the 1973 Earls Court Motor Show. Considering its humble beginnings, it was surprisingly elegant in the metal. It even had very modern touches, like rubber bumpers at a time when most cars still wore shiny chrome bumpers. Unfortunately, it failed to impress the management at British Leyland, who decided not to develop the design further, so this remained the sole example.

# Aston Martin Lagonda

Visitors to the London Motor Show of 1976 must surely have been startled by the new offering from the Newport Pagnell firm of Aston Martin: a William Towns-designed limousine for the super-rich. The Lagonda was handbuilt with a space-age interior laden with stunning gadgets, and was complete with the famous Aston Martin V8 which guaranteed speed to match its looks, at a price of £25,000.

Unfortunately, its reliance on state-of-the-art technology brought the company great embarrassment, as the first car to be delivered suffered computer failure and total shutdown in front of the world's press at Woburn Abbey.

We don't normally make cars like this

# Aston Martin Ogle Coupé

Aston Martin have produced several oddities throughout its history, one such car being the Ogle Coupé, built in 1972. Only two examples were ever made, and 50 per cent of the production total was written off in a road accident in 1979. Its bodywork, designed by Tom Karen, was made from glassfibre, while above its waistline, it was made almost entirely of glass. Inside, complementing its futuristic exterior, there was a head-up display of warning lights reflected in the windscreen, allowing the driver to pay attention to both the road and the vital functions of the car at the same time.

# Audi RSQ

Product placement works wonders for a brand, and car companies know that. Therefore competition can be fierce to get cars in prominent films, so when Audi were given the chance to make the star car for the film I Robot, set in 2035, they knew it had to be special. The car they designed was the RSQ; a car that was obviously an Audi, but came equipped with what we all hope to be familiar with in 2035. In place of wheels, there were spheres, while its two doors were rear-hinged to the C-posts of the body, and opened according to the butterfly principle.  Accurately predicting the future is notoriously difficult: only time will tell whether our cars will look anything like this.

# Austin 7 Swallow

Of the 336 different versions of Austin 7 built between 1922 and 1939, the Swallow must be among the most pretty. Launched in 1928, it was so called because the body was built by the Swallow Sidecar Company of Blackpool, later to become Jaguar Cars. Its elegant body brought coachbuilt standards to the humble Austin, and even featured a ladies' make-up face powder and mirror set inside the glove-box. It was available as either an open cabriolet or enclosed saloon.

# Bristol 412

Bristol is a company which has never built cars the way other companies do, and has survived by making exclusive cars in penny numbers for far longer than any other company, such as Jensen, for instance.

Their cars have always been hugely luxurious, and their handbuilt craftsmanship has been part of their charm. The 1975 412, however, was something of a design aberration, built in the decade that taste forgot. Not even its silky V8 engine, which could propel the car to speeds of up to 140mph, was sufficient to make up for the slab-sided grotesque bodywork, which made it the least desirable Bristol in the company's history.

We don't normally make cars like this

# Buick Le Sabre

To be fair to other cars from 1951, Buick's Le Sabre was a concept car that was never intended to go into production, but it featured such wonderful science fiction extras that actually worked, and this made it way ahead of its time.

A wrap-around windscreen may not sound too exciting now, but this was the first car ever to have one, and much more excitingly, it also had a rain sensor which, once triggered, would automatically raise the roof.

Designed by the great Harley Earl, its jet-fighter styling was revolutionary, and with a 335bhp V8 engine powering the magnesium and alloy-bodied car, it was no slouch either.

Happily, it still exists today, and wows onlookers with its styling, gadgets and sheer presence.

# Citroën 2CV 4x4 Sahara

The Citroën 2CV was famously invented for carrying a farmer across a ploughed field with a basket of eggs in the passenger seat without any harm coming to his delicate cargo. For most people this was enough, but a Citroën dealer, M. Bonnafous, believed there was a market for a 2CV that could carry on across still rougher terrain, and in 1962, he designed the Sahara. Subsequently it was taken up by Citroën and offered alongside the standard car.

Bonnafous's design was ingenious in simply installing a second engine in the car, driving the rear wheels. With one engine (the front) working alone, it was capable of 40mph, but with the second under power, a top speed of 65mph came within reach. Because the rear engine occupied the space where the fuel tank would normally go, and also because two engines meant a greater thirst, two petrol tanks were installed, one under each front seat. Similarly, the spare tyre was displaced, and found a new home on top of the bonnet, which all helped make the car look more rugged.

Two engines also meant a higher price, and this restricted its sales potential and in total, just 694 were built. Survivors today are highly prized among Citroën fans.

We don't normally make cars like this

# Citroën Bedouin

The Bedouin was based on a Citroën 2CV and was similar to the Africar designed and built by Tony Howarth. It was made in small numbers in Britain by Bob Williams of Special Vehicle Conversion. The crudely shaped body panels were made from resin-coated plywood and the roof could be removed to leave a Mehari-style open-topped 'Jeep'.

A cheap, fun Jeep alternative, it found more favour with Citroën devotees than anyone else, but demand was small, and few were built.

Citroën are one of the world's most idiosyncratic car manufacturers, and proudly French. Yet the Bijou was a British-designed and built (in Slough) Citroën, penned by Peter Kirwan-Taylor, designer of the Lotus Elite. Beneath its glassfibre two-door bodyshell lay the mechanicals of a 2CV, the car Citroën had failed to sell in any quantity to the conservative and wary British.

Unfortunately, due to the increased weight of the body, it was even slower than the 2CV, and in the five years from 1959, it sold just 207 examples, being heavily outclassed by the Mini, which was also cheaper than the ugly Bijou.

We don't normally make cars like this

# Fiat Jolly

The Fiat Jolly was a coachbuilt special made by Ghia of Turin, based on the Fiat 600, which was first launched in March 1955.

Many Jollies came with wicker seats and a fringed top that made the car look like an ice-cream vendor's van. The Jolly was attractive not only to the sort of people who might buy a normal 600 but fancied something different; it also found customers amongst the very wealthy, and Fiat boss Gianni Agnelli was a keen owner.

# Jaguar Owen Sedanca

The Jaguar Owen Sedanca, built by H.R. Owen and based on an XJ12, was launched in 1973, and despite its questionable looks, more than 100 orders for the car were reputed to have been placed. Very shortly after this promising start, however, the 1974 oil crisis hit, and the project very rapidly came unstuck. What was meant to be opulent, and with exclusivity guaranteed, failed to achieve even the modest hopes of its makers and in the end the grand total of just three cars was built, of which at least one is known to still exist.

Apart from the oil crisis, it is widely believed that Jaguar's refusal to back the project played its part in the car's failure. Jaguar was never going to support a venture like this, however, when they were only a year away from launching their own V12 coupé, the XJS.

We don't normally make cars like this

# MG Metro 6R4

The Austin Metro was launched at the beginning of the 1980s as a replacement for the Mini, and soon found favour with the 'blue-rinse brigade' as an easy, uncomplicated and undemanding car to drive. As a rival to either the Mini or the Ford Fiesta it was fatally flawed, but it sold well enough.

But then, in 1984, Austin Rover decided they wanted a car to go rallying, and set to work converting this unassuming 'shopping-trolley' into a fire-breathing Group B rally car. The result was a mid-engined four-wheel-drive, 400bhp near supercar, but strangely, still just recognisable as a Metro underneath all the spoilers, extended wheelarches and bodykits.

# Morgan Plus Four Plus

The Morgan Plus Four Plus of 1964 was a strange car from a peculiarly traditional company. Strikingly modern, the sleek body hid the standard Morgan chassis and underpinnings, but most startling of all was the fact that the Malvern company's traditional, hand-built body had been replaced by one made from glassfibre. Press and customer reaction alike were of a mind: this was not what a Morgan should be.

Fortunately for Morgan, they were small enough to be flexible and correct their mistakes early. It was quickly seen as a failure, and after just 26 examples were built it was dropped.

We don't normally make cars like this

# Nissan Land Glider

Have you ever been out driving, seen a corner coming, and thought to yourself, 'Gosh, if only my car could lean into the corner the way that motorcyclist does'? If you have, then you're not alone, because some of the visionaries at Nissan came up with the Land Glider for such a person. Launched at the 2009 Tokyo Motor Show, it's an electric concept car that can lean as much as 17° in corners, and the passenger sits behind a driver who has computer game controls at his fingertips rather than a normal steering wheel. The technology goes further: when it needs a recharge, it can be parked at a wireless recharge point, and its non-contact recharging does away with the need to plug a lead into it.

# Renault Avantime

The Renault Avantime was a bold step forward in car design, but as so often in the past, the public was not convinced by such daring. In its sole year on sale in the UK, just 190 examples found buyers, while in France, only 2,654 examples were sold.

While the Avantime was always intended as an exclusive statement which would mark its owners out as part of an artistically knowledgeable elite, such poor sales figures could not be sustained, and the design of the future was consigned to the dustbin of the past in a depressingly short time.

We don't normally make cars like this

# Rolls-Royce Camargue

As one would expect of a Rolls-Royce, the Camargue launched in 1975, and designed by Sergio Pininfarina, was opulent in the extreme, whilst at £29,000, cost 50 per cent more than the open-top Corniche. Unfortunately, it was an ugly car that lacked the grace of a Rolls-Royce.

It had a sophisticated independent self-levelling suspension system and a superb split-level air-conditioning system that cost more than a new Mini. Each car took six months to build, and left the factory at the rate of just one per week. During the 11 years it was in production, only 534 were ever built.

# Rolls-Royce Silver Wraith
## coachwork by Vignale

Ordering a brand-new Rolls-Royce is a very special occasion. No two cars are alike, and with an almost limitless choice of optional extras from which to choose, the chance to make your car a personal statement is there for every customer. Joseph Maschuch of New York, however, took the idea of personalisation further than most when he ordered his long-wheelbase Silver Wraith in 1954. He had the chassis shipped to the renowned Alfredo Vignale Coachworks in Italy, where they created this totally unique body that is most unlike any other Rolls-Royce. It came complete with a cocktail bar, a television and a toilet under the back seat, which was generally used for chilling champagne rather than its expected duties. Thankfully the car still exists, and is owned by the Blackhawk Collection in Danville, California.

# 7

We don't normally make cars like this

# Rover Whizzard

Rover had been interested in gas turbine engines since 1940, and had worked with Sir Frank Whittle in the development of his early jet engines for use in aircraft. After the war, Rover continued playing with the idea, eventually building a car using this technology.

The 1950 Rover Whizzard, nicknamed JET 1, was a heavily modified Rover 75, with a front-mounted gas turbine engine which reached 150mph in official tests, but could dispose of fuel in the most dipsomanic of fashions: it struggled ever to beat a miserable 5mpg. Rover however, continued to try to improve this thirst until 1965 when the accountants closed the books on this developmental cul-de-sac.

# Plastic fantastic

# Arawak Hustler

The Arawak Hustler, designed by Terry Tyrrell in the mid-1970s, was built in Antigua by Arawak Motors Ltd. Its ugly glassfibre bodywork housed an 875cc Hillman Imp engine and mechanicals. This was unfortunate, as it coincided with the Rootes Group back in the UK deciding finally to axe production of the Imp.

It is believed that less than 300 of these poorly proportioned pseudo-Jeeps were built before the supply of Imp parts ran out, and a subsequent attempt to rejig the car to accept Vauxhall Viva components was stillborn.

# Argyll

The Argyll was an ambitious project started in 1976, which struggled on until the economic crash at the end of the 1980s. It was a muscular-looking, albeit somewhat poorly proportioned, mid-engined coupé, which housed a turbo-charged Rover V8 engine mounted transversely behind the rear passengers.

With its box-section chassis clothed in a glassfibre body, it was not surprising that the Argyll was capable of impressive speeds, with a maximum in excess of 160mph being claimed. It was well finished and was sold as a luxury sports-coupé.

It proved unsuccessful, however, costing £7,000 more than a Ferrari 308, and very few were ever made.

# Bamby

The golden age of the bubblecar finished 20 years before Alan Evans, made redundant from his job in Humberside in 1982, set about trying to revive it with the Bamby, a car he based on a Peel 50 he owned.

His design, like the Peel (see page 93), had a single seat, three wheels, with the rear wheel powered by a 50cc Yamaha moped engine, which enabled him to boast of 100mpg, and this, combined with a gull-wing door, he hoped, would make it desirable. It was not cheap, however, at £1,597 and after building only 30 examples, the Bamby was killed.

The Yorkshire-built Biota from 1969–76 was a startling looking little car, whose glassfibre body, fixed to a space-frame chassis, hid the humble mechanicals of Alec Issigonis's masterpiece, the Mini.

Many Mini-based cars had ungainly front ends, a design feature militated by the Mini's tall engine, but the Biota skilfully avoided this by having a lower bonnet interrupted by a large bulge and air intake to hide the rocker cover. Clever design meant the Biota weighed just 8cwt, and this gave it a competitive edge in many areas of amateur motorsport. In seven years of manufacture, less than 40 were built.

**Plastic fantastic**

# Britannia GT

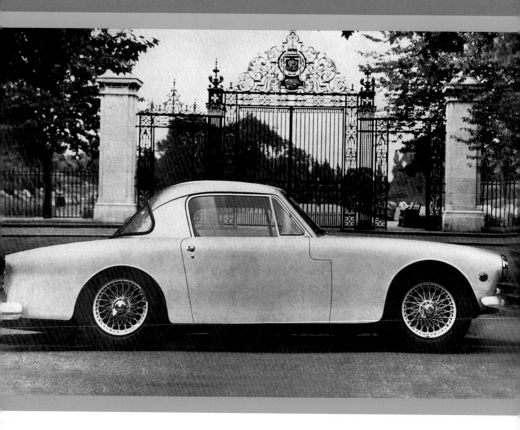

The Hertfordshire-based Britannia GT from 1957 was meant to be a rival to Aston Martin, coming so comprehensively equipped that there was no point in having an options list. It would offer 'a combination of characteristics never before available in one car at any price… limousine luxury, brilliant acceleration, superlative comfort, magnificent braking, impeccable handling, and exceptional luggage space.' Its engine was a 2,553cc unit from the Ford Zodiac, tweaked to 150bhp, fitted to a tubular chassis and enclosed in a glassfibre body.

Unfortunately, the car had an unrealistic price tag of £2,400 which was £400 more than the fabulous Jaguar XK150S, and after selling only six cars, the project was declared bankrupt.

# Chantecler

The Chantecler (Nightingale) was designed by Paul Vallée in France at the beginning of the 1950s as yet another take on the microcar theme.

Initially launched with a 125cc engine, this was later updated to 175cc. It had basic rubber suspension and tiny wheels, a bulbous glassfibre body and a folding hood.

Its dodgem-car looks did not attract many customers, and many who were persuaded to buy one were those too young to drive a real car as, in many countries, it was legal to drive one without the need for a licence.

# Cicostar

The Cicostar was an unusual-looking two-seat microcar built in France at the beginning of the 1970s.

Its glassfibre body was fixed to a steel frame chassis. The 50cc engine ensured it was available to drivers as young as 14, thus improving its sales potential, while a 30mph top speed was the pay-off. Its supposedly aerodynamic shape may have helped slightly with performance, but would not have won any marks for style in a beauty contest. Sold as 'the most elegant of little cars', and with automatic transmission passing power to the rear wheels, driving it was a doddle.

Rinspeed of Switzerland was the creator of the Eco 2 two-seater city car, which lasted for a short while at the beginning of the 1990s, using Ford Fiesta mechanicals including a 1-litre engine, five-speed gearbox, and a number of other components.

Its polypropylene body panels were fixed to the tubular frame in such a way that the frame tubes were visible externally, and although it was exceedingly short, the Eco 2 was not unpleasant to look at. Only a few were built however.

# Entreposto Sado

The little Sado, built by Portugal's Nissan Importer, Entreposto, for four years from 1982 in Lisbon, was noteworthy in part at least, because its name so accurately draws attention to the pathetic appearance of the microcar.

It followed the usual design of microcars, featuring a glassfibre body on a steel tube chassis, but was endowed with a 550cc Daihatsu engine, considerably bigger than most of its kin possessed, and this gave it a none too sad top speed of almost 70mph.

# Fuji Cabin

The pretty little Fuji Cabin was launched at the 1955 Tokyo Motor Show, at a time when competition for sales was extremely stiff.

The Cabin's bodywork was made of polyester and was very sleek. Its cyclops front and small luggage space to the rear were all part of its cute nature, and it was intended to be seen as a fully enclosed Scooter.

Unfortunately, enclosing a scooter added extra cost, and the end price was uncompetitive. In total, just 85 were made, of which three are known to survive.

# 8
## Plastic fantastic
# Fun Tech 50

Marketed as 'The moped that thinks it's a sports car,' the British-designed and built Fun Tech 50 with its maximum top speed of 30mph is designed with the 16-year-old in mind, while its larger brother, the 350, is aimed at someone with a full car or motorcycle licence, and is correspondingly faster. Both have a high-resistance polythene monoshell, alloy wheels and 12-volt electrics. The 50 is exempt from London's congestion charge.

# Futura

The startling Futura was designed by Robin Statham in 1971, who first showed his prototype at the 1971 Racing Car Show.

It had a very rakish, wedge profile, and most unusually, entry was through the front windscreen that hinged to one side. For all its futuristic looks, it was based on the humble floorpan of a VW Beetle, which should have helped it reach production. Development costs, however, which included resiting of the headlamps and passing all sorts of tests before it could go into production, killed both the car and the company, although subsequently, one was finally completed in 1979.

**Plastic fantastic**

# Invacar

The Invacar was launched in 1948 by Oscar Greeves. It was a three-wheeled machine powered by a 147cc Villiers engine based on a design he had drawn up for a paralysed cousin. With large numbers of war casualties requiring transport, Greeves was in the right place at the right time and with the right car and it was not long before the government was buying every Invacar he could build, and more besides. These were built by a number of companies including AC, Harding, Dingwall & Sons, Barrett, Tippen & Son, Coventry Climax, and the fabulously named Thundersley. The final Invacar was the DHSS Model 70, the design and production of which was shared with AC, who had had experience with a similar car, the Petite (see page 74). The last Invacar was supplied in 1977.

The curiously styled Kaiser Darrin KD161 was a glassfibre-bodied sports car built by Kaiser Frazer in Michigan, USA for a short time in the mid-1950s.

Apart from its weird appearance, which was not to everyone's taste, most notable was the way the two doors opened: rather than adopting a hinge mechanism like everyone else, the Kaiser Darrin's doors slid forwards. It also featured a fully disappearing soft-top, but it was not a success, and production stopped after just 435 examples had been built.

# Ligier Be Up

The idea of the microcar is an enduring one, which still has devotees even in the even in the 21st century. In 2003, French ex-Formula 1 team Ligier launched the Be Up. Priced at just under £6,000, this crazy little machine was styled by Giugiaro Design and consisted of a space frame chassis with polycarbonate panels fixed to it. It was powered by a 505cc twin-cylinder four-stroke petrol engine that developed 21bhp and transmitted its power to all four wheels by a CVT automatic transmission system.

In common with microcars of previous generations, it was available to drivers with only a full motorcycle licence rather than a full car licence, and was marketed to trendy young professionals looking for a fun car without the high insurance costs of a true sports car.

# Meister Kabine K6

The Meister Kabine K6 was built for a short while at the beginning of the 1970s at Graz in Austria. Its glassfibre body was fully enclosing and egg-shaped, seating its two occupants side-by-side. Fitted with a 49cc moped engine, it had four forward gears but no reverse, and in spite of its teardrop shape which made it look like it was capable of considerably more, its top speed was a disappointing and miserable 25mph.

**8**

*Plastic fantastic*

# Norsjo Shopper

Built in Forshagan, Sweden in the 1960s, the Norsjo Shopper from the front looks very much like a number of other microcars, except it appears the manufacturer ran out of glassfibre before completing the bodywork.

This bizarre little three-wheeler is steered by handlebars, kick-started like a moped, and is capable of 45mph flat out. The huge canopy, which is hinged to allow you to get in or on to it, must surely create aerodynamic havoc as the daft machine approaches its very modest top speed, however.

# Ogle 1.5

David Ogle ran a design consultancy business in Letchworth penning designs for radio and television sets before turning his attention to cars in 1959. His first attempt, the 1.5, used a Riley 1.5 floorpan and the BMC 1,500cc B-series engine, which propelled the car to a top speed of 90mph. Its pretty two-door sports coupé bodywork was made from glassfibre, but at £1,623 6s 3d, it didn't come cheap. Inside, the interior was trimmed in Connolly hide and deep-pile carpets, and for an extra £22 8s 6d a radio could be specified. Only eight 1.5s were built.

Plastic fantastic

# Opperman

The Opperman sounds and looks like a German offering rather than something British, but it was in fact built near Elstree, north of London, between 1956 and 1959. This was another 1950s attempt at cheap motoring, built to the usual recipe: glassfibre two-seater coupé body on a glassfibre platform, and propelled by a 322cc Anzani motorcycle engine.

The car was not endowed with the most pleasing of appearances, but it was miserly in its need for fuel, and at £265, it found customers for a short while, until the Mini showed the world how good inexpensive motoring could be.

# Quest

Designed by Derek Meddings in London for the 1968 film *Doppelganger*, the Quest should never really have gone any further. However, this was the sixties, and strangely, the fantasy car was turned into reality of sorts.

New moulds for the glassfibre body panels were made and new gimmicks were added to the car, including fibre-optic cables linking the headlights with the dashboard display to show the driver that all was well, and a 'guaranteed harmless' fascia filled with radioactive gas to provide 24-hour illumination. And the price? A staggering £3,000 – only three were ever built.

**Plastic fantastic**

# Runaground

The Runaground is the work of Poole-based car customiser Andy Saunders, whose fertile imagination has produced some of the world's weirdest one-off custom cars.

Starting out life as a Reliant Regal and a Monbar 146 speedboat, Andy saw the possibilities of producing a real head-turner in 1986 by combining the hull of the boat and chassis of the tired three-wheeler. With his father owning an MoT testing station, he was fully *au fait* with the regulations connected with making a car street legal, and the end result is a fabulous piece of road-humour.

# Siva Llama

In 1970, Neil Trickett designed the Mule, which was meant to be an update, using glassfibre bodywork, of the Mini Moke. Two years later, he updated this design further, renaming it the Llama. This used the engine and mechanicals from a Hillman Imp, and like the donor car, had its powerplant mounted at the rear.

It was hoped this strange looking machine would sell in the UK as a complete car, and in complete knock-down form for Third World countries. Unfortunately, it was a sales disaster and only 50 examples found buyers before the company went bust.

Plastic fantastic

# SP Highwayman

The SP Highwayman was designed and built by Derek Skilton and Jack Perkins of Hooe, in Sussex in 1972, who had previously specialised in restoring Bugattis.

Its angular body was sports inspired and paid homage to 1930s styling with the separate front wings and body, although one of the only two ever built, featured a most bizarre glass enclosure at the back which looked not unlike a small greenhouse. Its magnesium alloy Wolfrace wheels hinted at the power on tap from its Rover V8 engine, but it failed to attract any buyers, and the company failed after a couple of years.

# Status 365

The Status 365, so named because it was designed to be used every day of the year, was designed by ex-Lotus engineer Brian Luff in 1977. Using Mini subframes, engines and other components, the 365 was an ugly machine whose bodywork, built from glassfibre and plywood seated four people. It was a clunky design with little to recommend it, and attracted very few sales as a result.

# 8

**Plastic fantastic**

# Strathcarron

STRATHCARRON

The Strathcarron was blindingly fast and should have enjoyed greater success.

First seen as a concept in 1996, production got under way in the autumn of 2000. The car's 125bhp 1,200cc Triumph motorcycle engine was developed and tweaked by Strathcarron engineers, and accompanied by the Triumph's six-speed sequential gearbox, was fitted into an ultra lightweight Kevlar/carbonfibre body designed by the highly respected race engineers Reynard, who also designed the car's suspension. Bilstein springs and shock absorbers, AP racing brakes, OZ Gran Tourismo wheels and specially developed and treaded Yokohama tyres completed the package, which in total weighed a featherweight 1,213lb, and gave the car a staggering 227bhp per ton.

Unfortunately, unforeseen changes to the Single Vehicle Approval regulations effectively outlawed the use of motorcycle engines for volume producers, and as a result, the enterprise failed after less than 20 cars had reached their buyers.

The TiCi (pronounced titchy) was designed by furniture designer Anthony Hill in 1972. Its name hinted at its size; just 89in in length. The pretty little machine was described as mid-engined, with the engine and front subframe of a Mini placed behind the car's two occupants. The body was made from glassfibre, and was very much in the 'fun-car' mould.

Launched in 1972 as a kit costing £395, with doors and a hardtop available for a further £35, it deserved better success than it enjoyed – only 40 kits were sold before the imposition of VAT made it too costly.

# Trabant

Most car manufacturers are guilty, to a lesser or greater extent, of the crime of boasting and perhaps making slightly larger claims for their cars than can be supported by fact, but none is as guilty of brazen fabrication as were the manufacturers of the Trabant, calling it a 'limousine'. There can hardly have been a car ever produced less worthy of the name, with its pug-ugly Duroplast body, and its two-cylinder two-stroke engine, which left clouds of blue smoke everywhere it went, to remind those citizens of East Germany not yet lucky enough to own one, what a miserable machine it was. Nevertheless, in its defence, it must be pointed out that over 3 million examples were made and sold, compared with the Morris Minor, which only managed 1.2 million. Possibly the closed market may have helped…

Designed by a *Star Trek* fanatic in Illinois in 1989, the Trylon looked very space-age, but the reality was somewhat more down-to-earth and disappointing. Its rear end was powered by nothing more adventurous than a VW Beetle powerplant, although later some models could be specified with the engine from a Mazda RX-7. Many other components including steering, suspension and gearbox also came from the VW donor car, but in spite of this, there was much to fire the imagination if its humble mechanicals could be overlooked.

Its interior, for instance, was accessed by lifting the giant clam-shell canopy, seating the occupants tandem style, and the driver was entertained by a space-age dashboard and aircraft-style steering controls. Over 250 examples were sold either as kits or ready-assembled cars.

Plastic fantastic

# TX Tripper

The Tripper from 1970, was made by a firm which normally produced bath tubs, and used as its base the chassis and running gear from a Triumph Spitfire. It looked like a cross between a Beach Buggy and an open sports car, and used the 2.5-litre fuel-injected Triumph engine from the PI, which gave it highly respectable performance: 0–60mph in under seven seconds and a top speed of 120mph.

In spite of the power, its weird appearance did the Tripper no favours, and by 1979, when it was finally killed off, a total believed to be just 75 examples having been sold.

# Weird yet successful

# Ariel Atom

The Ariel Atom is a single-purpose car: it is a stripped-to-the-bone pure sports machine offering no frills, and scant weather protection. Its 220bhp VTEC engine, placed behind the driver for maximum grip and handling, ensures that there is always storming performance available on tap, virtually unhampered due to its minimalist chassis and bodywork.

Although road-legal, the Atom was designed very much with the racetrack in mind. It has plastic bucket seats and full four-point race harnesses, quick-release steering wheel, and as if to reinforce the sporting purpose, there is no ignition key – just a starter button.

# Atco Junior Trainer

With the introduction of the driving test in Britain in 1935, the business of motoring began to be taken more seriously, and Charles H. Pugh Ltd, the manufacturers of the well-known Atco lawnmowers, decided to do their bit, by helping make young children aware of road safety and the elements of handling a car, several years before they could experience the real thing.

The Atco Junior Trainer had one forward and one reverse gear, and was powered by a 98cc Villiers engine, giving a top speed of 10mph, and was aimed at schools rather than the wealthy private buyer.

# Biscuter

The Biscuter was designed by Gabriel Voisin and built in Spain by Autonacional of Barcelona, starting in 1953. Made from aluminium, it was a very basic and crude yet startlingly clever microcar, whose front wheels were powered by a 9bhp, 197cc Hispano Villiers engine. Its top speed, as guaranteed by racing driver Juan Manuel Fangio, was 48mph, helped no doubt by the fact that the entire car weighed only 528lb, and it sipped petrol at the rate of just 57mpg.

The Biscuter was remarkably successful, and by the time production ceased in 1960, a total approaching 20,000 of the diminutive town microcars had been built.

Launched in June 1970 by the Tamworth firm Reliant (who had acquired Bond two years earlier) the 700cc Bond Bug was twice as groovy as any three-wheeler deserved to be. It was a real 1970s style statement, alongside flared trousers, platform shoes, bushy sideburns and the Raleigh Chopper.

With striking lines penned by Tom Karen of Ogle Design, and its alloy wheels, the Bug was rakish, although its top speed was just 75mph. In essence, it was little more than a heavily reworked Reliant Robin, but its style was of the moment, and in total, 2,268 examples found groovy customers.

# Cub Commuter

The Cub Commuter was made in Taiwan exclusively for the American market, and was an extremely sleek-looking microcar, seating two people. Its 91in long body was made of glassfibre mounted on a steel chassis, and it was powered by a 400cc air-cooled four-stroke engine, which gave the machine a top speed of 50mph.

It was sold as the 'ultimate in driveability and convenience', and was marketed in the United States by Convenient Machines Inc.

# Cuno Bistram

The 1954 Cuno Bistram was a single-seater from Hamburg, which might be best compared to a child's pedal car, was never going to sell in large numbers looking the way it did, and so a sales total of 50 is surprisingly good.

Its appearance however, disguised a machine that was considerably more sophisticated than a pedal car, coming as it did with independent coil spring suspension attached to a ladder frame chassis. Its Ilo 150cc engine drove one rear wheel via a chain, and gave this weird machine a top speed of 45mph.

Weird yet successful

# Frisky

'As practical as it is beautiful' was the proud boast of the manufacturer at the launch of the Frisky, designed by Giovanni Michelotti and built in Staffordshire between 1956 and 1964. The dumpy little machine looked far better in the artist's impressions in the sales brochure, however, than it did in the metal and glassfibre.

In its favour, the Frisky was frugal (65mpg) and reasonably fast (65mph), courtesy of its 17bhp 250cc Villiers, two-cylinder motorcycle engine mated to a four-speed gearbox with reverse, which powered the wheels by a chain drive.

# GAZ Chaika

The GAZ Chaika (Seagull) was built in Gorki, USSR and launched in 1965. Its styling was very much influenced by Americana, and it came with a 5.5-litre engine, which propelled the behemoth to speeds of around 100mph, a result of the 195bhp on tap. Everything that could benefit from power assistance, such as steering, brakes, windows and even the radio antenna had this as standard, and here indeed was a most unegalitarian machine for carrying around some of the country's most prestigious comrades.

# Hustler

The Hustler, launched in 1978, was another design from William Towns. Its design was simple, featuring a sturdy chassis using standard Mini sub-frames and engines, all enclosed in neat glassfibre panels. Above the base chassis line, the almost infinite choice of body configuration allowed for a simple, clean-lined car, van, pick-up or even limousine. There were four, six and eight-wheeled versions, and even an amphibious variant, all built around the same basic chassis.

Remarkably, in total, there were 72 different variants of the Hustler by the time it finally reached the end of production, some 10 years later.

# King Midget

The King Midget company of Athens, Georgia, USA, was unusually successful by microcar standards, remaining in production for 22 years.

Its first car was a single-seater designed by aeroplane pilots Dale Orcutt and Claude Dry, which was launched in 1947. It was rear-engined, and very small indeed, with either manual or automatic transmission mated to a 6hp Wisconsin engine, and costing $270 in kit form.

Four years later, the second series Midget was introduced with a more practical two-seater roadster body redolent of a Jeep, and with an 8½hp engine.

Weird yet successful

# Nash Metropolitan

Most weird cars sold only in penny numbers, simply because they were too weird to appeal to public taste, but the Nash Metropolitan, in spite of being both unusual in appearance and hopelessly under-powered, sold over 104,000 units. Fitted with a 1,500cc engine, among its standard fittings were a radio and heater, and after 1958 it even had an opening boot.

Built in Britain, the car was aimed at the US market, where it was a great success, but those sold in the UK suffered terribly from lack of any rust-proofing, and its soft handling was not to British tastes either.

# Panther De Ville

Panther of Harlow, Essex built a number of 'replicars' such as the J72 Brooklands and the Lima, but the most expensive was the De Ville of 1974. Over the 11 years of its production lifespan, just 60 examples were built, with many of them going to very wealthy clients including Elton John, and even the Sultan of Oman, whose car had gold-plated fittings and a solid gold eagle mascot sitting astride the Bugattiesque radiator grille. The final De Ville was commissioned by HRH Prince Suliaman of Selangor in 1985. This six-door version came equipped with TV, video, glass divisions, electric seats etc. and cost £105,000.

# Project Flat Out

The name Andy Saunders is not unfamiliar to the lover of weird cars, and Saunders surpassed himself with Project Flat Out, turning an old Fiat 126 he had bought from eBay into the world's lowest car. As if building such a car – which for Guinness World Record recognition had to have a proper roof, be driveable and completely street-legal – weren't challenge enough, he chose to build it in three days in front of an audience of 33,000 people at the International Autojumble at Beaulieu in 2006, helped by two friends, Doug Brown and Jim Chalmers. It stands just over 21 inches high.

# Rocket

While looking like a 1950s racing car, the Rocket's performance is thoroughly modern. Its four-cylinder Yamaha FZR1000 motorcycle engine revs to a shattering 13,000rpm, delivering 143bhp from just 1,002cc. A top speed of 143mph may seem merely adequate for a car claiming to be a Porsche slayer, but its 0–60mph sprint time of just 3.9 seconds illustrates more vividly the thrills that can be found at the helm of this most unusual machine. Weighing just 882lb is not only an advantage in the power stakes, it also contributes significantly to its barely believable handling capabilities.

# Stout Scarab

Bill Stout of Dearborn, Michigan, was another designer whose earlier work in the aircraft industry helped him arrive at some startlingly unique shapes. The 1932 Scarab was a beautiful, aerodynamic sedan, whose rounded shape eschewed the need for bonnet or boot.

Over the course of 14 years he built several versions of essentially the same design, with the first being bodied in duralumin, most in steel, and the last, built in 1946, being one of the first cars to have a glassfibre body. They all had engines at the rear, and although undeniably handsome, never made it into serious production.

# 10

# Petrol not required

There have been many attempts at finding alternative fuel sources for cars, and experiments continue even today, but none has exceeded the weirdness of the Arbel from France, which boasted a Genastatom nuclear reactor as its power source.

For 1958, this was a car virtually from science fiction: it had headlights which switched on and off automatically, ashtrays that emptied themselves (onto the road), a windscreen washer which was filled by rainwater, and an 'electric-drive' transmission and braking system.

A lavish brochure was produced, but shortly afterwards this most unusual of machines disappeared leaving many unpaid creditors.

# BMA Hazelcar

Electric cars have been part of motoring since the very early days, and with very few exceptions, all have failed miserably, for a variety of reasons. The 1952 BMA (Battery Manufacturing Association) Hazelcar from Hove in Sussex, however, was not one of those happy exceptions.

Its open two-seater body was made from aluminium and it came with a 2hp electric motor powered by nine six-volt batteries, and was capable of 20mph over a 60-mile range. Costing £535, it was doomed to failure from the outset, and only six were ever made, one of which still survives.

# California Commuter

The startling appearance of the California Commuter is nothing compared with its achievements, as it holds the world records for real-world fuel efficiency for both petrol and diesel-powered vehicles. Its inventor, Doug Malewicki, drove it from Los Angeles to San Francisco and achieved the astonishing figure of more than 157mpg on the journey on 20 November 1980.

Funded by dentist Bill Long, the Commuter was designed specifically for record breaking on public roads, and can therefore be considered a proper, if somewhat unusual car. Weighing just 230lb, the diminutive three-wheeler was steered by two inter-linked joysticks. Plans for building your own version are available on the internet for just $29.95.

# Car-Cycle

Built originally in 1986 as an experimental prototype, American Bob Stuart's Car-Cycle was a Kevlar-bodied, lightweight, three-wheeled, human-powered vehicle.

Its weird shape housed an adult, a child and two bags of groceries, and subsequent improvements included a small electrical motor to supplement the rider/driver's efforts. Steering was by side sticks with approximately 2ft of travel, which ensured that the action was not so direct that the vehicle would twitch when under control.

Equipment included a windscreen wiper, a fan to cool the driver on hot days, headlight, brake light and three lights that flashed up and down in time with the pedal movement, located in the 'safety-sail'.

Despite considerable media interest and press coverage, the project, perhaps unsurprisingly, failed to attract interest from industry, and the hoped-for production never materialised.

# Corbin Sparrow

Launched in 2001 as the Corbin Sparrow Personal Transport Module, this electric three-wheeler from California is striking to look at, and while still burdened by the Achilles' heel of all electric vehicles – poor range (30–60 miles) – it is at least capable of a decent top speed, reaching a highly respectable 70mph.

Designed by Mike Corbin, its composite body is designed for only one person, measures 8ft 4in, and like most electric cars, is highly unusual in appearance.

The Electra King was built by the B&Z Electric Car Co. of Long Beach, California, but a car less deserving of the title 'king' is hard to imagine.

Looking very much like a three-wheeled invalid carriage, later up-rated to four wheels, but otherwise unchanged in form, the Electra King was on sale for over 20 years from 1961, and was one of the longest-lived and most successful of all electric cars. The range was only about 45 miles, while a top speed of 30mph was another limiting factor, but it was used by people purely for local shopping trips in preference to walking. During its production lifespan, its sale price rose from $2,180 to $3,395.

Petrol not required

# Electraction Rickshaw

Throughout the history of electric vehicles, range has always been the major problem, and the Electraction Rickshaw, complete with its full dose of seventies' chic was no different.

It was designed by Roy Haynes in 1977, who had previously worked for the rather more successful Ford Motor Company in a similar capacity, and with its trendy van-without-roof styling, alloy wheels and a hood which looked like it had come from a pram, it toured the various motor shows.

Its 55-mile range and top speed of just 30mph ensured it found no purchasers, as being intended for recreational use, such performance was wanting, and thus another electric hopeful soon fizzled out to nothing.

# Electric Jester

Jester by name, but most definitely not by results: this little electric two-seater can be seen beetling around the leafy lanes and the towns of the New Forest doing everything any other car might do, but much more cheaply and greenly.

The Jester is a huge step forward in electric car technology and at recent official tests it proved its range to be a staggering 200 miles between charges (about the same distance many petrol cars go between refills), and it is capable of 70mph. At present this wonder car is not on sale.

# Enfield Electric

The Enfield 8000, to give its correct title, was a dumpy-looking Noddy car from 1976, whose vast weight was supposed to be offset by an aluminium body fitted to a space-frame chassis. All the usual problems associated with electric cars of this era (poor range, low speed, colossal weight and the high cost of replacing batteries) were present in the 8000.

While a Mini could be bought for £1,000, the Enfield cost £2,802, and sales were thus predictably poor. Of the 103 cars built, only 42 went to private owners, with the rest being bought by the predictably sympathetic Electricity Council.

# General Motors EV1

For most of the electric car's history, it has been championed by well-meaning but usually drastically under-funded individuals, and apathy from the world's motor manufacturers has kept it on the sidelines.

General Motors was the first of the big companies to put serious effort into trying to solve the problems of weight and range that have always dogged the electric concept, and the 1996 EV1 was a major step forwards, offering a range of up to 130 miles. It also had a top speed of 80mph, and could reach the first 60mph in less than nine seconds.

The EV1 was a serious car, and came fully equipped with airbags, traction control, ABS, air-conditioning, electric windows, cruise control and stereo. Its bodywork was made from composite panels fixed to an aluminium structure, and it had an enviable drag coefficient of just 0.19.

Petrol not required

# Jet-Powered Reliant Kitten

The Kitten represented a hoped-for break into the mass market for the Tamworth firm of Reliant in the 1970s, having one more wheel per car than was their norm. Unfortunately, the breakthrough never came, and most Kittens have gone the way of other 1970s cars and are long since scrapped.

One example, however, is not able to enjoy a quiet retirement, as Ivon Cooke, its owner, installed an Auto Diesel STAD 250 gas turbine engine. Idling at 15,000rpm, its maximum revs are a staggering 27,000, it uses kerosene as its fuel, and is capable of 100mph.

# Kesling Yare

Some of the strangest cars have been designed and built by people from completely unrelated professions, such as the 77-year-old dentist, Dr Kesling from Westville, Indiana. His futuristic, glassfibre-bodied, electrically powered, diamond-formation, four-wheeler of 1978 richly deserves the title 'weird'. Entry was via a single gull-wing door, and the six lead-acid batteries gave it a range of 35–40 miles at a pleasing top speed of 55mph, a figure no doubt helped by its supremely slippery shape. Only one example was ever built.

Petrol not required

# MIA Electric

Whilst the MIA Electric looks like another concept car that is 'exploring the bounds of the possible', the reality is that it is a real car, available to buy and drive on real roads if funds and the fear of being ridiculed are not an issue. With the driver sitting in the middle – and no doubt comforting himself with the thought that the owner of a McLaren F1 enjoys the same driving location – the strangely unfinished-looking car is capable of 68mph and has a range of approx 80 miles, although not if the top speed is often reached. Its makers claim it is ideal for such duties as the school run, which surely indicates they are unfamiliar with the full emotional impact of sulking children forced to travel in something they fear their friends will mock them for.

# Mochet Velocar

Almost unique in a world of weird cars, the Mochet, built in France, had no power source at all: the majority of cars built by Charles Mochet being adult pedal cars. However, for a short period at the end of the 1920s, the lazy could buy a Velocar equipped with a 142cc engine, but for the most part, the car relied on its driver for motive power, and as such, became highly prized among priests, doctors and commercial travellers during the Second World War, when no petrol was available for anything other than military purposes.

# MOTA

Sometimes, hindsight is of no benefit at all. One such example is that of the MOTA, a car that in all probabilities never left the drawing board, and for good reason: the claims made by its would-be manufacturers were just too wild to support. For here was a car that had no internal combustion engine at all; rather, it was powered by its 'patented Polade Power plant'. Apparently 'motivated by the magnetic forces which produce the speed of light, the MOTA delivers flashing acceleration, breath-taking speed, the pile-driving power of steam' etc.

The sales brochure promised much, and it is impossible now to judge whether it was all just a scam or whether the Banning Electrical Products Corporation of Saginaw, Michigan really believed they had an idea worth putting into practice. The reality is that the dream car of tomorrow is still waiting for tomorrow to come…

# Pasquali Riscio

The Italian Pasquali Riscio, launched in 1998, was yet another electric car where the designers, because it did not have an internal combustion engine, did not feel constrained to make their car look like it had, and so went off to produce something so daft in appearance, that its sales potential must surely have been adversely affected.

It was available in single or two-seater versions, but to drive the latter version a driving licence was required. It was supposedly capable of a 35-mile range at 25mph from its 24-volt power supply, but was only really intended for city use.

# Peel Trident

The Isle of Man-based firm of Peel concentrated on making very small cars with even smaller engines, and of great interest to the student of weird cars must surely be its 1965 Trident, whose glassfibre body was topped by a Perspex dome with a flat screen at the front. This dome formed part of the huge (relatively speaking) hinged canopy through which access to the two-seater interior was gained.

Costing just £190, most Tridents were three-wheelers, powered by a 49cc moped engine giving 100mpg fuel consumption, but a few were built as four-wheelers and these were powered by an even more frugal electric motor.

# Pohlmann EL

The 1981 Pohlmann EL had a drag coefficient of just 0.25, and with a separate electric motor driving each rear wheel, was capable of a very respectable top speed of 70mph. It carried two adults who entered the sleek glassfibre one-box body through gull-wing doors.

The development of the Pohlmann was sponsored by the Rheinish-Westphalian Electricity Works, whose financial support hid the costs of building 30 examples. A long hard look at the books, however, showed it was too expensive to expect any commercial success, and the project was subsequently shelved.

# Pumpkinseed

Saving fuel is the aim of most drivers, but using no fuel at all is for most still a distant dream. The Pumpkinseed was a car built in Santa Cruz which used not only solar power, but cleverly also made use of wind power, with its two vertical operable wings which were able to supply approximately 50 per cent of the car's power in a 12–15mph crosswind.

A competitor in the Darwin–Adelaide World Solar Car Championship, the Pumpkinseed was driven at speeds of over 60mph, but no outright top speed has ever been verified. Driving requires a whole new array of techniques to be learnt, as steering is by foot, the wings are operated by the right hand, while the brakes and throttle, are both rather confusingly, operated by the left hand.

The world is now used to the idea of hybrid petrol-electric vehicles, with cars such as the Honda Insight and the Toyota Prius available commercially, and others promised. Back in 1981, however, things were different and the whole idea was still very much in its infancy.

Built on a VW Beetle chassis, the Quincy-Lynn Hybrid had an 8hp engine which helped keep the batteries charged, and increased the range of the futuristic-looking, plastic-bodied, lightweight car to around 100 miles. Known as a 'charge-depleting' hybrid, this technology has now been completely superseded, but was seen as revolutionary at the time, and was a necessary evolutionary step towards the current and future versions of hybrid cars now available.

**Petrol not required**

# Renault Twizy ZE

When Renault first unveiled the Twizy ZE concept car at the Frankfurt Motor Show in 2009, it attracted a fair amount of attention, as any vehicle looking this unusual would. But Renault went further, claiming they would build it for real, and put it on sale for real people to buy and use on real roads.

True to their words, Renault have produced it in largely unaltered form, although sadly the cladding on the wheels hasn't made it to production reality. ZE stands for Zero Emissions; the holy grail of carmakers keen to be seen as good world citizens, leaving the power stations that charge its lithium ion batteries to do the polluting instead of the car.

# Sebring-Vanguard Citycar

The Sebring-Vanguard Citycar was an ugly, electric vehicle, built in Maryland, USA during the 1970s, and which sold surprisingly well considering its utilitarian and sparse appearance. Such sales success can only be credited to the fears during that decade for fuel crises.

Looking like a cheap European microcar, this two-seater used a 48-volt 3.5hp electric motor which gave its occupants the opportunity to travel 50 miles per charge at a rate of up to 38mph.

# Sinclair C5

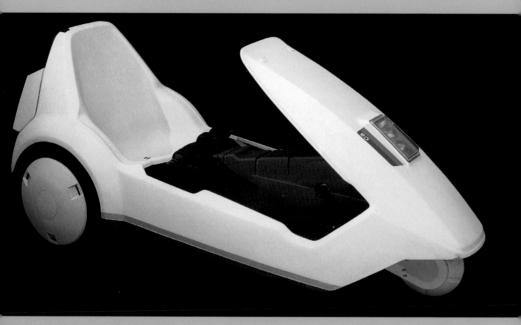

People from all kinds of professions over the years have tried their hand at car designing, with widely varying degrees of success, and so it should come as no surprise to see the undoubted genius of Sir Clive Sinclair having a go.

His idea, the C5 of 1984, was essentially a good one, making an electric vehicle capable of 15mph that could be used on the roads by people as young as 14 without the need for driving licence, insurance, road tax or MoT. Its three-wheeled chassis wore the world's first polypropylene body, and the 20-mile range could be significantly enhanced by pedal assisting it up hills. The launch price was £399 but this was soon greatly reduced, and although around 12,000 were made, few buyers could be found in the UK, with many being sold abroad after the enterprise had collapsed.

Fears about other road users not being able to see the low-slung vehicle made for nervous owners, and in the end, these concerns, fuelled by media scare stories, killed support for the ill-fated vehicle, and plans for larger models were scrapped.

With the Second World War in full swing, one of the earliest casualties to normal life was the availability of petrol for private use. While most owners put their cars in storage for 'the duration', an inventive few looked for alternative fuels, and the easiest to source was electricity.

The Story, from Holland, was a flimsy little two-seater whose 1.3hp motor propelled its occupants to a none-too-electrifying 15mph, over a range of approximately 35 miles. Although the first 50 sold quickly, the inability to acquire the materials to build many more soon killed off the project.

Petrol not required

# Teilhol Citadine

The Teilhol Citadine was an electric three-wheeler built in France in the 1970s that looked very much like a cross between an Isetta bubblecar and a piece of cheese. Entry to the unlikely machine was through the front, as in the Isetta, but there the similarities ended, as its electric power led to a quieter journey, while the occupants must surely have needed thick skins to be able to live with the constant level of mirth the weird contraption must have generated everywhere it went.

Launched in 1995 as a 'slim-line vehicle for independent thinkers', the Twike is an electric tricycle designed in Switzerland, whose 5kW motor can be assisted by pedals to add to its range, extending it to up to 55 miles. When a recharge is necessary, it can be plugged into an electric socket and charged at the rate of 1km per minute.

Its occupants sit side-by-side in the ultra-light bodyshell, which is made from thermoplastic panels fixed to an aluminium space-frame chassis. Steering is by joystick, and other features include an on-board computer, cruise control and regenerative braking.

With the Witcar, one has the feeling that more effort went into the concept of free transport for the good people of Amsterdam than into designing the vehicle itself.

Looking not entirely unlike a mobile telephone kiosk or shower cubicle, the three-wheeled electric car was available to anyone who joined a scheme operated by the Amsterdam authorities whereby users were given a magnetic key and could use the weird machine anywhere within the city, plugging it in to a charge point at the end of their journey so that it would be ready for its next user. The co-operative that owned and operated them was wound up in October 1986 and the vehicles put into store. These were later sold for scrap, but a few escaped for display in museums.

# CHAPTER ELEVEN

# Let's just be different

# Aurora

The 1957 Aurora, arguably the ugliest car ever built, was the brainchild of Fr Alfredo Juliano, an American Roman Catholic priest.

His idea was to make a new kind of safety car, and his creation boasted all kinds of unique features such as a windscreen so shaped that its reverse slope improved visibility during rain, and needed no windscreen wiper. There were huge amounts of padding in the car, seatbelts and a telescopic steering column, while its body was made of glassfibre, and featured roll-over bars built into the 'astrodome roof'. Priced at $15,000, it found no buyers, and Fr Juliano ended up in jail after being found guilty of accounting irregularities. Fortunately, the car survives.

# Beauford

The Beauford was a truly weird design launched in 1985. There, in the middle of a long chassis, was the unmistakable shape of a Mini bodyshell, mated to a long bonnet and surrounded by long flowing wings aping the infinitely more graceful shape of a 1930s tourer.

The mechanicals were from a Ford Cortina, and the engine could therefore be anything from 1.6 litres up to a 2.8-litre V6. While classic car enthusiasts were not convinced by the faux styling, it quickly found its niche as a wedding car, and subsequently spawned other designs on a similar theme.

# BMC Sphynx

An automatic winner in any 'weirdest-looker' competition, the BMC Sphynx, almost incredibly, considering its size, was a one-off built for the demanding sport of hill-climbing, in which it took part just once.

Remarkably little is known about this huge green behemoth, beyond the fact that it was built by Gilbert & Rickard of Syon Hill Garage, in Isleworth, London at the beginning of the 1970s and was funded by the two Suppan brothers in Switzerland. Its centre wheels did the driving, powered by a Downton-tuned BMC 1,800cc 'Landcrab' engine, which ensured that the beautiful, hand-shaped aluminium two-seater body, complete with its gull-wing doors, would be quick off the mark. It must be assumed that problems came from the diamond formation wheel pattern, which may have made it difficult to steer, especially against the clock in a hill-climb.

Happily, the car survives, and its current owner has plans to restore it to full working order.

When Romano Artioli resurrected the Bugatti name, aiming to build the ultimate exclusive sports car, this seemed entirely in keeping with the marque's heritage.

Called the EB110 – EB for Ettore Bugatti, and 110 as the car was to be launched on what would have been his 110th birthday, in 1991 – it was a superlative supercar whose V12 engine would give it a top speed of 212mph. Its looks, however, were open to debate, with many believing it was just outrageously ugly.

In the end, costs ran away with the project, and it is believed 139 cars were built before the company was declared bankrupt.

# Davis

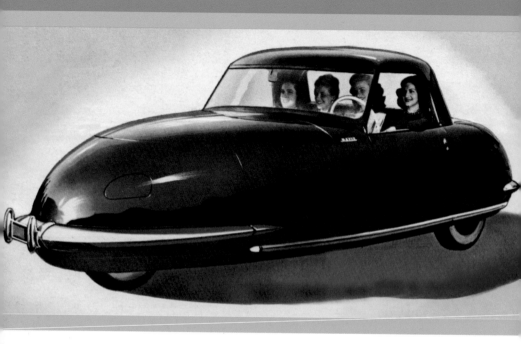

The 1947 Davis took the design of three-wheelers to an entirely different plane. As a prototype design it was very striking and bold, and made all the right impressions. It was over 15ft long and able to carry four adults side by side on its bench seat. Its designer, Gary Davis from California made a number of extravagant claims including a top speed of 116mph and fuel consumption of 30mpg from its 2.2-litre four-cylinder engine, and on the strength of this, he signed up a number of dealers which brought him $1million in franchise fees.

Although a total of 17 were built, production never got under way seriously, and Davis was subsequently jailed for fraud.

# Dobbertin Surface Orbiter

By and large, we're used to the idea that cars are for roads, although we generally don't have much of a problem accepting that a good number of them are OK on the rough stuff too. There are even a few that have been able to get by on water, with varying degrees of success. But Richard Dobbertin had a greater vision than any car featured in this book. He decided he wanted to build a vehicle that could quite literally go around the world, regardless of terrain – or indeed lack of it. Starting with a 1959 Heil milk tanker, he invested some 14,000 man-hours in converting it into the Surface Orbiter, and the result is a machine that has now covered more than 33,000 miles on land and 3,000 miles on water, often in mountainous seas. Its 6.5-litre diesel V8, fed from a 340-gallon tank, is capable of 70mph and can get through fuel at a rate of 10mpg on land and 1-2mpg at sea.

# Dunkley Pramotor

Dunkleys of Birmingham were manufacturers of prams, when in 1922, they launched the Pramotor, the last word in the pampering of nanny and child. Available with a 1hp or 2½hp engine, the Pramotor was a motorised platform resembling the rear half of a scooter that fitted to the back of a Dunkley pram, and on which the nanny would stand. Controls for the throttle and brake were then fitted to the rear handle of the pram. The engine was kick-started – as elegantly as possible in a nanny's uniform – and the machine was ready for the road. Whether the road was ready for such a contraption is not recorded, but being a motorised vehicle, it was no longer legally permitted to use the pavement. It was extremely expensive, however, and very few were sold.

# Gaylord Gentleman Coupé

The Gaylord Gentleman Coupé was an ambitious, if unorthodox-looking car that was extremely short lived. The bizarre bodywork was the work of designer Brook Stevens, while the chassis was designed by Ed Gaylord. In total, only four were built, in 1956, including the prototype, which was subsequently scrapped.

Although US designed and funded, the three production cars were built by Zeppelin in Germany, featuring Cadillac V8 engines, retractable hard-tops and variable-assist power steering.

Many car designers try to imply speed in the shape of their creations, but few can ever hope to realise this aim more fully or successfully than hot-rod builder Bill Carter achieved with his mid-1980s car which he called G-Whiz.

The engine and much of the running gear came from a V12 Jaguar, while the striking canopy came from a Hawk jet trainer. Inside, clever touches such as a cut-down Quartic (almost square) steering wheel from the Austin Allegro added further to the feelings of flying a jet aircraft, while comic touches included the fitting of two chromed beer barrels for fuel tanks.

# Helicron

Like the Leyat, featured in Chapter 1 (see page 17), the 1932 Helicron was a French design. This example, thought to be unique, was found in a French barn in 2000 and has since been restored. It now resides in the Lane Motor Museum in Nashville, Tennessee. Whilst much of the car is original, its engine is from a relatively modern Citroen GS, and the propeller is linked directly to it. Speed up the engine, therefore, and the prop will go faster, pulling the car forward faster. Most remarkably, the car has passed a French safety inspection and is actually licensed for use on French roads, according to its owners. Steering is by the rear wheels, and whilst luxuries would seem to be relatively few on the Helicron, a fully 'air-conditioned' ride is guaranteed, complete with flies, bugs and general road grit.

# Hooper Empress

The emergence of Bentley from under the shadows of Rolls-Royce during the 1980s and 1990s has been remarkable, and the marque now boasts a highly desirable range of elegant sporting cars. In 1987, however, before the launch of the Continental R, they did not have a two-door coupé, and the well-known coachbuilder Hooper stepped in to fill the gap, offering a rebodied Turbo R.

Called the Empress, it had the right price, £275,000, but had the brash looks of a boulevard cruiser built in Detroit rather than the restrained elegance one would expect from Bentley.

The Berline from 1953 was a weird design whose aircraft roots were immediately obvious, and while some may have thought this was just the French take on a Messerschmitt, it had one crucial and very unusual difference.

Its makers, the aircraft company SNCAN, equipped the car with front wheels mounted on outriggers which could be folded in and underneath the fuselage style body, allowing the car's width to shrink by 18in to just 3ft, thus enabling the car to taxi to a 'landing spot' on the inside of a garden gate.

# Lea-Francis Ace of Spades

The Lea-Francis Ace of Spades was an improbable design that aimed to provide owners with 1988 technology wrapped in the cloak of a 1930s shape and appearance. It used a Jaguar six-cylinder engine placed in a sturdy chassis and enclosed in an aluminium body featuring flowing wings and running boards, while inside, the occupants were treated to the usual overdoses of forestry and hide. Unfortunately, components such as Austin Metro Van den Plas headlights detracted from the luxury appearance it aspired to, and ultimately the car was unconvincing. Only six examples were ever built, selling for £68,000 each.

# Litestar Pulse

The Litestar Pulse was built over a five-year period in Michigan by the Owosso Motor Car Company, during which time they completed just 347 of these amazing vehicles. Classified as a GCRV (Ground Cruising Recreational Vehicle), in essence it was a motorcycle with a small outrigger wheel on either side to stop the machine falling over, although only one of these outriggers would be in contact with the ground at any time. As the speed of the machine increases, the gyroscopic effect of the main wheels would remove the need for either outrigger. Although they only sold in penny numbers, those who bought one are fiercely proud of their machines, which are capable of speeds in excess of 130mph, whilst returning more than 70mpg.

# Marcos Mantis

Marcos was set up in 1959 by Jem Marsh and Frank Costin. Their early cars used marine plywood for much of the chassis and were always noted for their speed and ability to compete, and when in 1970, they introduced the weirdly shaped Mantis, it came with high expectations.

It used the 2,500cc straight-six petrol injection engine to good effect, and the car was a most luxurious machine, even when bought as a kit. Only 32 examples were sold, however, before the company went into receivership, but has since been revived on more than one occasion.

# Martin Aerodynamic

The science of aerodynamics has occupied the minds of many car designers from, in some cases, remarkably early on in the lifespan of the car's development, with varying levels of success. In 1932 the Martin Aircraft Company of Garden City, New York, decided to have a go at combining their aviation experience with the science of car design, and the strangely proportioned Aerodynamic was the result. In fact, only three prototypes were ever built, and whilst the disciplines of aerodynamics can be plainly seen in details such as the pontoon-shaped under-body, fully-covered rear wheels and a deep-sloping front with the body tapering towards the rear, what is clearly missing is the understanding of what makes a good-looking car. The depression of the early 1930s put paid to any further development of the concept, but fortunately this example survives and is on display at the Lane Motor Museum in the USA.

## 11

Let's just be different
# Messerschmitt Tiger

Known in their native Germany as 'Cinderella's Coffin', the 1958 Messerschmitt Tiger was a uniquely different car designed by Fritz Fend. Most of the Messerschmitts were three-wheelers, but the four-wheeled Tiger was the car to aspire to. Fitted with a 500cc air-cooled vertical twin engine which developed 20bhp located behind the rear passenger, who, in turn sat pillion-style behind the driver. The super-light machine was capable of speeds up to 75mph. Only 400 were ever built.

# Mohs Ostentatienne Opera Sedan

The Mohs Ostentatienne Opera Sedan, at $25,000, was designed as an exclusive American luxury car with all sorts of unnecessary extras, including a refrigerator, gold trim inside and velvet upholstery.

Most luxury cars are aesthetically pleasing, but the 1968 Mohs, however, was not. From its ugly chrome grille at the front, through to its oversized wheels with nitrogen-filled white-wall tyres, the list of design *faux pas* seemed almost endless. It was built on an International Harvester chassis and powered by a truck engine. Steel safety beams ran the length of the ungainly body, preventing any doors being placed in the car's flanks, so in their place, a single door rose from the roofline at the rear. Only one example was ever made.

# Mollmobil

The Mollmobil was a most unusual-looking machine, designed by Fritz Gorke in 1924, and built in Germany by Moll-Werke. This strange, tandem-style two-seater gave the impression of being built from the wreckage of a beach hut, and without anything but the most cursory design inputs from Herr Gorke. It was powered by a DKW engine of less than 200cc, and the resultant lack of power can only have added to the silliness of its appearance, although, as it had brakes of only the most fundamental nature, this may after all have been no bad thing.

# Neander Pionier

The 1934 Neander Pionier was designed by Ernst Neuman-Neander, a German artist whose interest in car design went back 20 years before penning this most striking of two-seaters. Its occupants sat one behind the other, tandem style, while its front wheels were powered by a 1-litre motorcycle engine that required no differential, and all was clothed in a deliciously different, Bauhaus-influenced body made from aluminium.

Although the Pionier looked like a one-off concept car about two decades ahead of its time, a small number were made and sold.

# New Map KV

Complete with a 125cc engine, unusually built by the company, the ugly 1938 New Map KV from France had a steel body devoid of any styling merit. This four-wheeled machine had a top speed of 40mph, but only in dry weather as, bizarrely, drive was transmitted to just one of the rear wheels by a rubber capstan rubbing on the tread of the tyre. Presumably, hill-climbing on a wet day was not something to be undertaken in the KV, whether or not the driver had brought a new map along. Surprisingly, in spite of its crudeness, approximately 2,000 were sold.

The Opus-HRF (standing for Hot-Rod Ford) was an immediate success (by custom car standards). Modelled on American-style T-bucket hot-rods, but built in Warminster, Wiltshire from 1966, it was scaled-down and anglicised sourcing much of its running gear from the Ford Anglia with the engine coming from the Ford Cortina 1600E. The cost of the car in kit form was just £99, which included the chassis, body and radiator shell. When finished, and weighing just 8cwt, it promised owners a 0–60mph sprint in just seven seconds according to the manufacturer's figures. Over 250 examples were sold, many of which were heavily modified to give extra performance.

Let's just be different

# Panther Six

The 1977 Panther Six looked like it had just rolled off the set of an episode of Gerry Anderson's *Thunderbirds* TV series. Panther had every hope that it would deliver equally improbable performance figures, for here, they claimed, was going to be the ultimate car: a top speed of 200mph from its 600bhp V8 engine, in an open-topped car, unbeaten in luxury as well as performance.

Its body was made from hand-rolled aluminium, while it also boasted on-board fire extinguishers in the engine bay, and the very latest in digital dashboard displays. Only two were ever built.

# Pininfarina BMC 1800

Remember the ugly BMC 1800, commonly known as the 'Landcrab'? While it was surprisingly capable in certain forms of motorsport (Prince Michael of Kent drove one in the London to Mexico Rally and got most of the way there), it was never a car that appealed to anyone on looks or style, and was deeply unsexy.

And yet, it could have been so different, if only BMC management had gone with Pininfarina's design study, for here was a sleek outline with hints of Citroën SM about it, and which would have been streets ahead of all in its class. Although the story for the 1800 had no happy ending, it would appear that the BMC management, under their subsequent BL name, appear to have used the shape as the basis for the David Bache-designed Rover SD1, which, despite being fatally flawed by poor build quality, was a stunner of a car.

# Quasar-Unipower

Unipower was a company based in Perivale, Middlesex, which built small sports cars using the A-series Mini engine to good effect, and the cars sold well. Then, one day in 1968, they were approached by Vietnamese-born fashion designer Quasar Khanh, who wanted a bold vehicle that would be guaranteed to attract publicity for one of his clients in Paris. To stand out in the fashion capital of the world, he needed something really extraordinary, and the resulting Quasar-Unipower fulfilled this brief admirably.

Built on a chassis using modified Mini running gear including an automatic gearbox, the cuboid, fully glazed vehicle exposed its occupants to the gaze of all around, and it goes without saying that visibility in the Quasar was particularly good. Even the seats were made from see-through inflated plastic, and entry to the interior was through one of the sliding patio doors fitted to either side. As a city car, which was, after all, where it was designed to do most of its work, it was faultless, with a turning circle of just 13ft. Its top speed of 50mph was doubtless a result of its not unsurprisingly poor coefficient of drag, but with the car being so short and tall, its ride at such speeds must surely have been extremely bouncy, and terrifying, especially for any passenger who dared to contemplate what the effects of even a small accident might be. Its minuscule dimensions (5ft 4in by 5ft 6in) must have been an asset in traffic, over which its passengers would have had no problem seeing, as they were seated high up in the glasshouse which took the car's height to over 6ft.

Possibly the biggest surprise was that further examples were not commissioned by manufacturers of double-glazing for promotional purposes. In total, only six cars were built, and it is not known if any survive.

# Reyonnah

The Reyonnah was a remarkable French machine whose fuselage body seated two in tandem, with the passengers getting into the car via a hinged perspex canopy, just like in a Messerschmitt bubblecar

Powered by a 175cc engine, this little cocktail of eccentricity from 1950 would have been enough to qualify as weird, but its party piece was altogether more startling: both its front wheels were mounted on outriggers, and could be folded under the car so that they matched the track of the narrowly spaced rear wheels and allowed it to go through gateways, or park in unfeasibly narrow spaces.

# Rinspeed Presto

Just occasionally, a car comes along that answers a question no-one had ever thought to ask, and we're left wondering whether it is a good idea or not.

One such vehicle is the Rinspeed Presto, a concept car that actually shrinks to fit the parking space. At the press of a button, the 12ft long four-seater will shrink into a two-seater (after the rear passengers have got out) measuring about 3ft less. To do this, the high-tech Pre-Peg Composite plastic body manages without doors, and the shrinking/expansion is carried out by electric motors.

# Rinspeed X-Trem

The X-Trem from Rinspeed of Switzerland, was weird on many levels, the most obvious of which was its outrageous appearance. Although only a concept car fitted with four-wheel drive and a 5.5-litre 347bhp V8 engine from a Mercedes M Class, it was capable of doing much more than most concepts, which look interesting, but do not actually work.

Allegedly, to provide assistance where even four-wheel drive could not, the X-Trem had a small integrated hovercraft for travelling across swamps etc. A number of issues appear not to have been addressed by the designers, principally amongst them being: what was the point?

The weird-looking 1948 Tasco (the initials of The American Sports Car Company) was designed by the famous designer Gordon Buehrig who was responsible for the Auburn 851 among others, and looked very much as if it belonged on a *Flash Gordon* film set.

The front wings were made from glassfibre and actually turned with the front wheels when steering, while much of the rest of the design drew heavily on aircraft influences. Unfortunately, the consortium that funded the project ran out of finance before it could go into production and it went no further.

The Vannod was another weird car that had its four wheels placed in a diamond formation, with both the rear and front wheels steering, and the middle two in charge of the driving. Propulsion came from a 200cc, 10bhp Sachs engine, which was mounted at the rear of the car, behind the two passengers. The driver, sitting further forward, sat alone in a central position, where the bodywork was tapering in towards the car's nose.

With two-tone paintwork and white-wall tyres, the good-looking Vannod was presented at the Paris Salon of 1958, but was not seen thereafter, and disappeared completely.

The Volpe (Fox) was an Italian microcar whose designers had tried just that little bit harder to design something approaching the styling of a bigger machine, and the end result was most pleasing. Launched in 1947, it was powered by a 6hp two-stroke engine of 124cc, which gave a top speed of not much under 50mph. Its two occupants sat in a stylish open body, and the car really deserved a better fate than its very short life, which ended in legal battles and lost deposits.

# Appendices

# Bibliography

*A-Z of Cars 1945–1970* Michael Sedgewick & Mark Gillies, revised by Jon Pressnell, Bay View Books 1993

*A-Z of Cars of the 1980s* Martin Lewis, Bay View Books 1994

*The Beaulieu Encyclopaedia of the Automobile* Edited by G. N. Georgano, The Stationery Office 2000

*Best Loved Cars of the World* John Plummer, Sackett & Squire Ltd 1979

*Cars Cars Cars Cars* S.C.H. Davis, Hamlyn 1967

*The Car – Its History – How it Works – The Great Marques* Consultant editor Maurice A. Smith, Hennerwood Publications Ltd 1979

*Cars of the Stars* Jack Scagnetti, Jonathon David Publishers Inc. 1974

*Cars That Time Forgot* Giles Chapman, Paragon 1997

*The Centenary Encyclopaedia of Automobiles* Graham Macbeth, Newnes Books 1984

*The Complete Encyclopaedia of Motor Cars 1885 to the Present* Edited by G.N. Georgano, Ebury Press 1970

*Dream Wheels* Chris Rees, Anness Publications Ltd 1998

*The Encyclopaedia of the World's Classic Cars* Graham Robson, Salamander Books 1982

*The Fun Car Explosion* Peter Filby, Bookstop 1979

*Kleinwagen* Edited by Matthias Dietz, Benedikt Taschen 1994

*The Observer's Book of Automobiles* Edited by L.A. Manwaring, Frederick Warne & Co. Ltd 1964

# Acknowledgements

The author wishes to extend his grateful thanks to all those listed alphabetically below for their encouragement and contributions both in terms of research and the use of pictures in this book.

Alex Campbell
Andy Saunders
Ariel Motor Company
Barry Stimson
Bertone
Bob Stuart
Caroline Johnson
Chris Rees
Citroën
Citroënet
Clwb-y-meicrocar
Combidrive Ltd
Cycleshop.com
Daimler Chrysler
Doug Malewicki
Ford Motor Company
Fun Tech
Gibbs
Giles Chapman
Hugh Kemp
John Visscheddijck
1000aircraftphotos.com
Jonathon Day
Malcolm Parsons
Malcolm Thorne
Manuel Costa e Meida

Mark Hughes
Microcar museum.com
Mike Worthington-Williams
Moller.com
Neils Marienlund
Nick Georgano
Nick Topping
Oldwoodies.com
Paul Griffin
Peter G Jones
Peter Nicholson
Pinifarina
Richard L Barksdale
Richard Rahders
Rinspeed
Rumcars.org
Tim Dutton
Tim Medeck
Tony Burchnall
Tony Foale
Twike
Steve Green
Vicki Garrison
WaterCar
3wheelers.com

# Index